COZY COTTAGE & CABIN DESIGNS

UPDATED 2ND EDITION

200+ Cottages, Cabins, A-Frames, Vacation Homes, Apartment Garages, Sheds & More

CRE▲TIVE
HOMEOWNER®

CREATIVE
HOMEOWNER®

Let *Cozy Cottage & Cabin Designs, Updated 2nd Edition* allow you to escape to that special place; the perfect small home placed in your favorite setting. Whether high atop a mountain, nestled along a lake shore, or situated on a sandy beach, all of the dwellings in this book are small homes designed for efficiency with each and every one having 1,200 total square feet or less of living area. Browse the floor plans, and find the ideal home that embraces everything you need for a comfortable and tranquil haven.

TABLE OF CONTENTS

WHAT MAKES A GREAT VACATION HOME?

The sound of waves crashing in the distance, or the gentle rustle of fall leaves making their way to the ground. Whichever sight or sound beckons you to take time away from your everyday life and discover a life less stressed, seek that special place. Most people can immediately picture the perfect setting that soothes their soul and takes them to a place where they instantly feel more at peace. But, besides the outdoor setting for the perfect getaway home, what features make it a great vacation getaway?

ENHANCE THE EXPERIENCE OF LIVING IN A SPECIAL PLACE

EASY ACCESS

Expansive decks that surround an entire home like the one shown to the right and below, provide easy access outdoors from any room. This allows homeowners to feel unified with their surroundings, which is almost always the main attraction in these special getaways.

RUSTIC, COZY TOUCHES

Also, the use of stone and dark wood trim creates a feeling of rustic charm. Warm and cozy, guests will never want to leave their surroundings when decorated with these details. Or, build a stone fireplace that adorns the main living space. Not only will it be beautiful, but it can provide an alternative heat source that will be sure to draw people in.

LIGHT & BRIGHT

Large dormer and picture windows make taking in views easy. Large windows offer a classic, alpine retreat compelling views, while still making the home feel like a private oasis tucked high in the mountains.

SEAMLESS TO THE OUTDOORS

A covered deck, like the one shown to the right below, is a great outdoor retreat. Perfect for alfresco meals, it allows outdoor enjoyment without the intensity of direct sunlight, making it perfect for sunbelt regions, beach, or coastal homes with tropical temperatures practically all year-round.

BREEZY BEDROOMS

Well-lit bedrooms with oversized windows not only permit sunlight, but help stir beach front breezes into interior spaces. With the use of beach accents, a bedroom like the one below is a cheerful, sunny retreat.

Many of these characteristics allow the natural beauty that surrounds your vacation home to shine.

Whether it's a cozy stone fireplace, a shaded covered deck, or a breezy beach side bedroom, these features will take your vacation home to a new level of relaxation and tranquility and lure you back time and time again.

CABINS

Plan #C20-163D-0004 is found on page 16.

Often blending perfectly with nature, cabins evoke a feeling of smaller, rustic living that works especially well in the rugged outdoor wilderness. Whether tucked close to a soothing stream or placed high in the snowy mountaintops, a cabin is the ideal small dwelling for getting away from it all. Typically, simple in style and decor, a cabin will always feel inviting and offer the perfect escape from everyday reality. Whether you're cozied up by the fireplace, or roasting marshmallows over an outdoor fire pit, cabin life will definitely create fond memories and moments of complete and total relaxation.

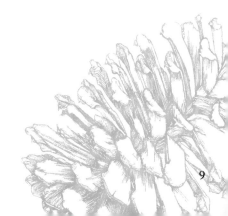

YELTON CABIN

If you're looking for a small, modern dwelling, or would love to escape city life but still have all of the amenities city life has to offer, then the Yelton cabin is for you. Soaring ceilings overhead will keep your special escape bright and cheerful. The openness promotes fun and easy entertaining when friends are over. You will be thankful for the large covered porch for those days when there's a mist in the air. This small home is far from boring and has everything you want!

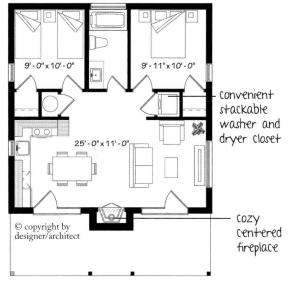

9' - 0" x 10' - 0"

9' - 11" x 10' - 0"

25' - 0" x 11' - 0"

convenient stackable washer and dryer closet

© copyright by designer/architect

cozy centered fireplace

PLAN #C20-032D-0813

686 square feet of living area
width: 26' depth: 26'
2 bedrooms, 1 bath
2" x 6" exterior walls
monolithic slab foundation standard;
crawl space or floating slab available for a fee

HUNTER'S WAY CABIN

The Hunter's Way cabin is the definition of rustic simplicity meets effortless style all with an open floor plan. A vaulted beamed ceiling tops the living room, dining area and kitchen for a spacious, open feel you will love. The open-concept floor plan allows the kitchen and dining space to blend perfectly with the main living area. The bedroom enjoys close proximity to the pampering bath featuring a shower and a free-standing tub in one corner.

combined kitchen, living, and dining areas

DECK

| WALK-IN | BEDROOM 2 9-8 X 8-10 | | DINING ROOM 10-10 X 12-4 |

KITCHEN 10-10 X 8-10

LIVING ROOM 12-0 X 12-4 EXPOSED BEAMS

BATHROOM

MASTER BEDROOM 13-10 X 12-0

FOYER

first floor 1102 sq. ft.

COVERED PORCH

© copyright by designer/architect

plenty of room for expansion

11'-6" × 11'-4"

15'-5" × 28'-2"

11'-6" × 10'-0"

optional lower level 1102 sq. ft.

PLAN #C20-032D-0932

1102 square feet of living area
1102 bonus square feet
width: 38'   depth: 30'
2 bedroom, 1 bath
2" x 6" exterior walls
basement foundation standard;
monolithic slab, floating slab or
crawl space available for a fee

REDMOND PARK CABIN

Feel like you've really escaped the hustle and bustle in the rustic Redmond Park cabin featuring a multi-purpose living/dining room that is up to the challenges of evolving cabin activities. Designed for relaxed living, this cabin enjoys access all around its perimeter onto a large wraparound deck. Setup your grill on one side of the deck, and designate an area to sunbathe on the other. Plus, the second floor studio will make a perfect artist's retreat, home office, or a private escape great for taking in views from a private outdoor balcony.

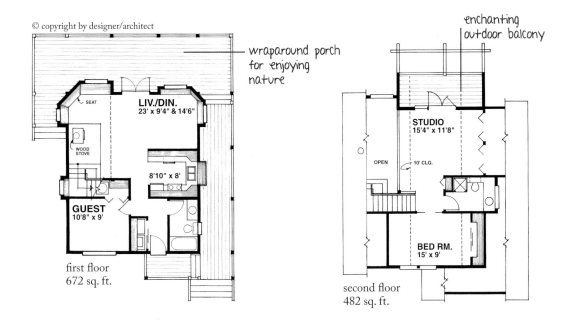

wraparound porch
for enjoying
nature

enchanting
outdoor balcony

LIV./DIN.
23' x 9'4" & 14'6"

SEAT

WOOD
STOVE

8'10" x 8'

GUEST
10'8" x 9'

STUDIO
15'4" x 11'8"

OPEN

10' CLG.

BED RM.
15' x 9'

first floor
672 sq. ft.

second floor
482 sq. ft.

PLAN #C20-080D-0004

1154 square feet of living area
width: 36'   depth: 42'-6"
2 bedrooms, 2 baths
2" x 6" exterior walls
crawl space foundation

CUB CREEK CABIN

Live a life of leisure in the Cub Creek cabin. Craftsman details give this small home tons of personality. Enjoy your morning coffee on the roomy covered porch, or grill up some burgers when it's time to barbecue. Inside, you'll find an open gathering space with a fireplace and many large windows for enjoying surrounding views. After a busy day in the wilderness, retreat to the comfortable bedrooms, each with their own bath.

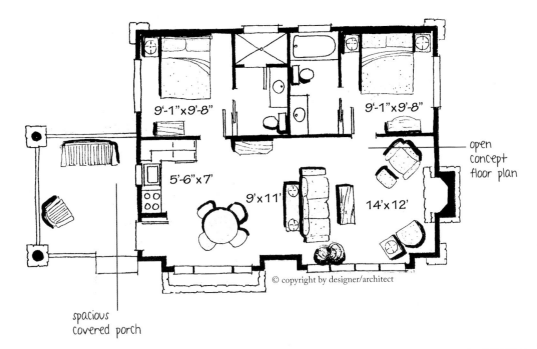

9'-1"x9'-8"

9'-1"x9'-8"

5'-6"x7"

9'x11'

14'x12'

open concept floor plan

© copyright by designer/architect

spacious covered porch

PLAN #C20-163D-0004

681 square feet of living area
width: 40'   depth: 22'
2 bedrooms, 2 baths
2" x 6" exterior walls
crawl space or slab foundation,
please specify when ordering

PARSON PEAK CABIN

You'll never want to leave the Parson Peak rustic cabin. The open interior has tons of windows for admiring surrounding views. Two bedrooms are near a full bath with a freestanding tub and a walk-in shower for added and unexpected luxury. Those sitting at the sizable island in the kitchen can easily keep up with what is going on in the living room. And, if you suddenly want to venture outside, then the quiet deck off the back is easily accessible and will be the place for you.

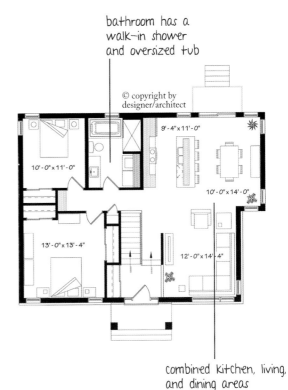

bathroom has a walk-in shower and oversized tub

© copyright by designer/architect

9'-4" x 11'-0"

10'-0" x 11'-0"

10'-0" x 14'-0"

13'-0" x 13'-4"

12'-0" x 14'-4"

combined kitchen, living, and dining areas

PLAN #C20-032D-0835

1146 square feet of living area
width: 40'   depth: 30'
2 bedrooms, 1 bath
2" x 6" exterior walls
basement foundation standard;
floating slab available for a fee

ADIRONDACK CABIN

The Adirondack cabin's vaulted great room is a pleasant surprise upon entering the home. The large and open space creates a great place for gathering since it combines with the dining area and kitchen. The center island in the kitchen offers extra dining space as well as a functional spot for preparing or serving meals. The grilling porch off the great creates useful covered outdoor living space. A handy laundry room and half bath are found off the hall tot he bedroom. Although small, the Adirondack cabin has everything you need!

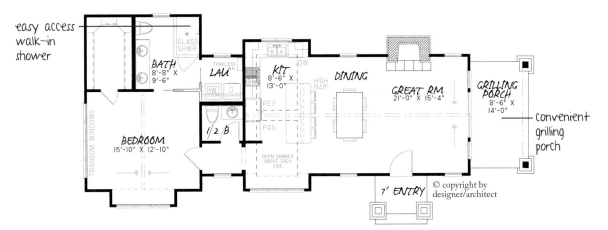

easy access walk-in shower

BATH
8'-8" X 9'-6"

GLASS SHWR

LAU

TANKLESS W/H

W D

1/2 B

KIT
8'-6" X 13'-0"

DW

REF

PAN

HIGH BAR

DINING

GREAT RM
21'-0" X 15'-4"

GRILLING PORCH
8'-6" X 14'-0"

convenient grilling porch

BEDROOM
15'-10" X 12'-10"

TRANSOM WINDOWS

OPEN DORMER ABOVE EACH SIDE

7' ENTRY

© copyright by designer/architect

PLAN #C20-155D-0214

1008 square feet of living area
width: 60'-3"   depth: 25'-4"
1 bedroom, 1½ baths
crawl space or slab foundation,
please specify when ordering

RHAPSODY CABIN

The Rhapsody cabin offers a quaint covered porch that greets guests as they arrive and provides a cozy area to sit and enjoy the sights and sounds of the surrounding outdoors. Spacious rooms throughout this home create a casual and open atmosphere. The kitchen and dining area combine for easy entertaining, and they are just steps away from the living room. The master suite on the second floor provides a private oasis that is sure to be appreciated by the homeowners.

© copyright by designer/architect

BA 2

BEDRM 2
8-10 x 9-4

UP

large, open living space

LIVING
13-8 x 15-2

KITCHEN
7-6 x 9-4

COV'D PORCH

DINING
9-4 x 9-4

first floor
650 sq. ft.

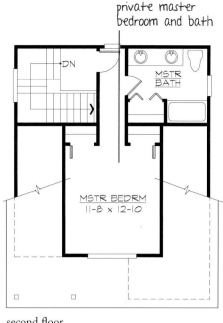

private master bedroom and bath

DN

MSTR BATH

MSTR BEDRM
11-8 x 12-10

second floor
350 sq. ft.

PLAN #C20-071D-0014

1000 square feet of living area
width: 24'   depth: 30'
2 bedrooms, 2 baths
2" x 6" exterior walls
crawl space foundation

SUNSET KEY CABIN

Take time out at the Sunset Key cabin. Whether lakeside or near the shore, cabin living in the Sunset Key will not disappoint. Unwind in the sun-filled floor plan with a fireplace in the living room. Or, retreat outdoors to the deck for mealtimes or to enjoy your coffee. The bedroom offers a restful spot for a good night's sleep, and is handy to the bath. If you need to do a load of laundry, then the closet for a stackable washer and dryer is right near the bath. There's also an office if an zoom meeting occurs, or you have email to respond to. But, don't worry, life will remain easy-going in this cabin!

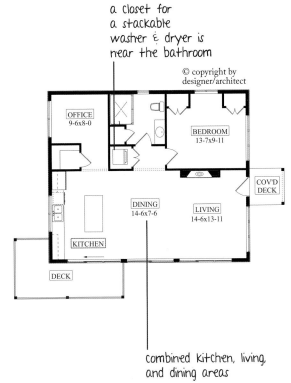

a closet for a stackable washer & dryer is near the bathroom

© copyright by designer/architect

OFFICE
9-6x8-0

BEDROOM
13-7x9-11

COV'D
DECK

DINING
14-6x7-6

LIVING
14-6x13-11

KITCHEN

DECK

combined kitchen, living, and dining areas

PLAN #C20-101D-0155

952 square feet of living area
width: 34'   depth: 28'
1 bedroom, 1 bath
2" x 6" exterior walls
slab foundation

PARSON GROVE CABIN

Enjoy the beauty of the backwoods in the Parson Grove cabin. With its expansive covered front porch, sitting around after a day of fishing or hiking will be a pleasure there. You'll be amazed when you step inside and discover the vaulted great room creating such a spacious feel to the interior. The kitchen with an eating bar for five people is entirely open to the great room, too. Everyone will be thankful for the cozy fireplace. Even though this cabin is small, it provides great comfort and function.

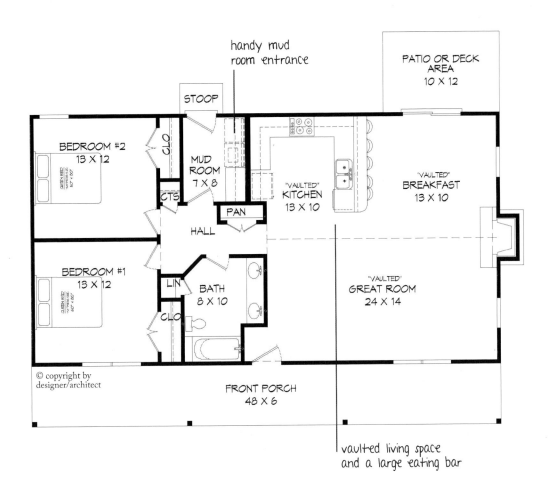

handy mud room entrance

STOOP

PATIO OR DECK AREA
10 X 12

BEDROOM #2
13 X 12

CLO

MUD ROOM
7 X 8

CTS

HALL

PAN

"VAULTED"
KITCHEN
13 X 10

"VAULTED"
BREAKFAST
13 X 10

BEDROOM #1
13 X 12

LIN

BATH
8 X 10

CLO

"VAULTED"
GREAT ROOM
24 X 14

© copyright by designer/architect

FRONT PORCH
48 X 6

vaulted living space and a large eating bar

PLAN #C20-141D-0013

1200 square feet of living area
width: 50'   depth: 33'
2 bedrooms, 1 bath
slab foundation standard;
crawl space, basement or walk-out
basement available for a fee

CROSSWOOD CABIN

The Crosswood cabin is an excellent starter home for any family. The living room boasts a handy coat closet located near the front entry. The efficient kitchen/dining area includes a side entrance to the outdoors, a closet that is perfect for a pantry, and a convenient laundry closet, so there is not a shortage in storage! The lovely master bedroom features a walk-in closet and private access to the bath. There sure is a lot of function for a smaller-size home!

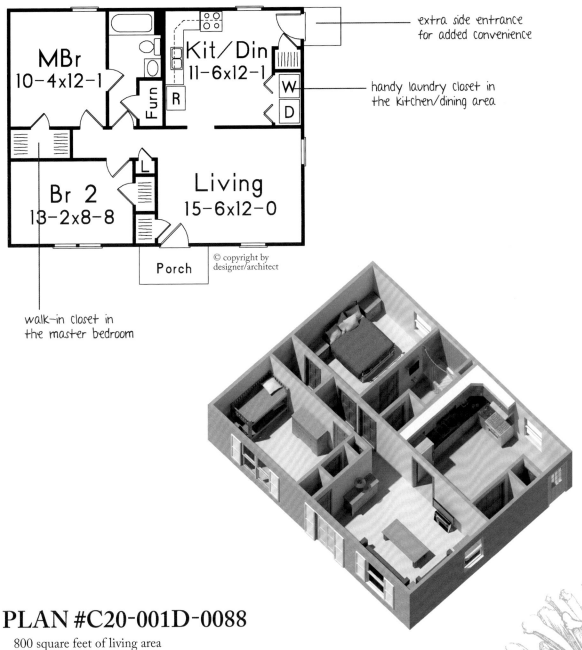

MBr
10-4x12-1

Kit/Din
11-6x12-1

Furn

R

W

D

Br 2
13-2x8-8

L

Living
15-6x12-0

Porch

© copyright by
designer/architect

extra side entrance
for added convenience

handy laundry closet in
the kitchen/dining area

walk-in closet in
the master bedroom

PLAN #C20-001D-0088

800 square feet of living area
width: 32' depth: 25'
2 bedrooms, 1 bath
crawl space foundation standard;
slab available for a fee

CHRISTY MEADOW CABIN

Rustic cabin living was never as comfortable as it is in the Christy Meadow cabin thanks to its very open floor plan, a front covered porch, and a rear covered patio. The conveniently located master bedroom has a walk-in closet, covered porch views, and direct access into the bathroom. Two additional bedrooms are located on the second floor.

PLAN #C20-111D-0033

1157 square feet of living area
width: 36'   depth: 38'
3 bedrooms, 2 baths
slab foundation standard;
crawl space or basement available for a fee

comfortable outdoor living area

© copyright by designer/architect

COVERED PATIO

WIC

BA 1

DINING
8²x9⁴

KITCHEN
9⁰x9⁴

MASTER BEDROOM
11⁰x12⁸

LIVING
17⁶x13⁸

WIC

COVERED PORCH

first floor
819 sq. ft.

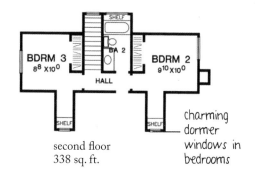

SHELF

BDRM 3
8⁸x10⁰

BA 2

BDRM 2
9¹⁰x10⁰

HALL

SHELF

SHELF

second floor
338 sq. ft.

charming dormer windows in bedrooms

CATHY CREEK CABIN

PLAN #C20-111D-0032

1094 square feet of living area
width: 40'   depth: 37'-6"

3 bedrooms, 2 baths

slab foundation standard;
crawl space or basement available for a fee

Rustic style at its finest in the Cathy Creek cabin. Breathe easy on the front covered wraparound porch with stairs that lead to a detached garage. Blended spaces create an area that feels larger than its true size. Three bedrooms provide enough space for family comfort.

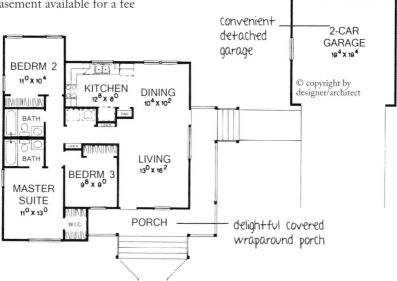

convenient detached garage

2-CAR GARAGE
19⁴ x 19⁴

© copyright by designer/architect

BEDRM 2
11⁰ x 10⁴

KITCHEN
12⁸ x 8⁰

DINING
10⁴ x 10²

BATH

BATH

MASTER SUITE
11⁰ x 13⁰

BEDRM 3
9⁸ x 9⁰

LIVING
13⁰ x 16²

W.I.C.

PORCH

delightful covered wraparound porch

CRANE POND CABIN

PLAN #C20-155D-0100

970 square feet of living area
width: 24' depth: 56'-6"
3 bedrooms, 1 bath
crawl space or slab foundation,
please specify when ordering

Life in the Crane Pond cabin will be harmonious. There's plenty of space for everyone with its three bedrooms and centrally placed bathroom. Barbecue time will be a thrill on your very own grilling porch. After grilling, settle into the screened entry porch and dine outdoors free of pests. The living and dining spaces are vaulted for a more open feel. The kitchen has a sizable laundry room nearby providing additional storage and space for chores. Whether a weekend escape, or a year-round residence, the Crane Pond promises a life less hassled.

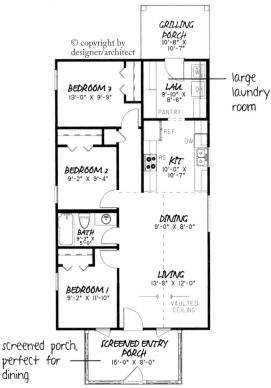

© copyright by designer/architect

GRILLING PORCH
10'-8" X 10'-7"

large laundry room

BEDROOM 3
13'-0" X 9'-9"

LAU.
9'-10" X 8'-6"

PANTRY

REF

DW

BEDROOM 2
9'-2" X 9'-4"

RG KIT
10'-0" X 10'-7"

BATH
9'-2" X 5'-0"

DINING
9'-0" X 8'-0"

BEDROOM 1
9'-2" X 11'-10"

LIVING
13'-8" X 12'-0"

VAULTED CEILING

screened porch, perfect for dining

SCREENED ENTRY PORCH
15'-0" X 8'-0"

PROVIDER II CABIN

PLAN #C20-001D-0040

864 square feet of living area
width: 36'   depth: 28'
2 bedrooms, 1 bath
crawl space standard;
basement or slab available for a fee

The Provider II cabin is the perfect rustic design for a woodside getaway. The cabin's L-shaped kitchen with convenient pantry is adjacent to the dining area for easy mealtimes and cleanup. This cabin also has easy access to the laundry, linen, and storage closets. Both of the bedrooms also include ample closet space for keeping everything organized. From the moment you enter, you will call this place home!

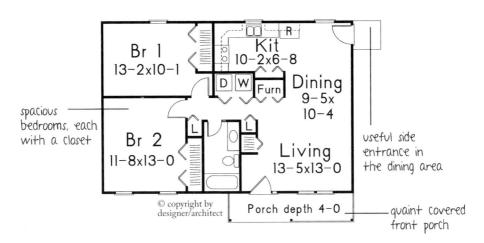

Br 1
13-2x10-1

Kit
10-2x6-8

spacious
bedrooms, each
with a closet

Br 2
11-8x13-0

Dining
9-5x
10-4

Living
13-5x13-0

useful side
entrance in
the dining area

Porch depth 4-0

quaint covered
front porch

© copyright by
designer/architect

MOHICAN CABIN

Step into this fantastic Modern cabin and find a floor plan that's easy to come home to. Sleek and open, the Mohican Modern cabin has an amazing see-through fireplace that warms both the living area and the bedroom equally. The main gathering space has two walls of towering windows for great views of the outdoors. The kitchen has an efficient layout that includes a handy side door to the outdoors in the side yard, and a closet that houses the washer and dryer in a convenient location. The center island finishes off the design and offers prep space, a double sink, a dishwasher and casual dining space. This Modern marvel is your ideal getaway spot!

PLAN #C20-126D-1012

815 square feet of living area
width: 30'   depth: 30'
1 bedroom, 1 bath
2" x 6" exterior walls
basement foundation

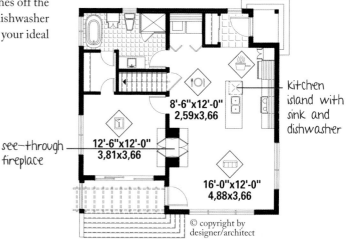

Kitchen island with sink and dishwasher

8'-6"x12'-0"
2,59x3,66

see-through fireplace

12'-6"x12'-0"
3,81x3,66

16'-0"x12'-0"
4,88x3,66

© copyright by designer/architect

WOODSMILL CABIN

PLAN #C20-007D-0042

914 square feet of living area
width: 30'   depth: 33'
2 bedrooms, 1 bath
basement foundation

Perfect for a sloping hillside waterfront lot, the Woodsmill cabin offers a quaint and comfortable dwelling with a living room that includes a cozy fireplace. The dining area has a sunny bay window, an open staircase, and a pass-through style kitchen creating an open interior throughout, while the lower level includes generous garage space and a finished laundry and mechanical room.

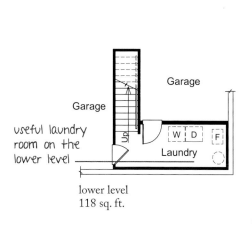

useful laundry room on the lower level

lower level
118 sq. ft.

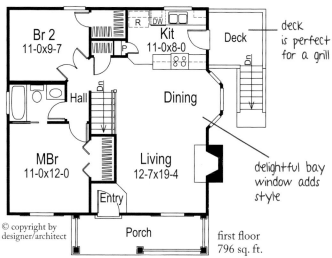

deck is perfect for a grill

delightful bay window adds style

Br 2
11-0x9-7

Kit
11-0x8-0

Deck

Hall

Dining

MBr
11-0x12-0

Living
12-7x19-4

Entry

Porch

© copyright by designer/architect

first floor
796 sq. ft.

LANAWOOD CABIN

The Lanawood cabin features a spacious living room that connects to the efficiently designed kitchen with a convenient raised snack bar. The lovely kitchen and bedroom both access the rear porch as well as the covered or screened porch, offering exceptional outdoor living comfort whatever time of day or season. A handy bonus room can be utilized as a hobby room or second bedroom.

PLAN #C20-077D-0008

600 square feet of living area
width: 31'-8"   depth: 26'
1 bedroom, 1 bath
basement, crawl space or slab foundation, please specify when ordering

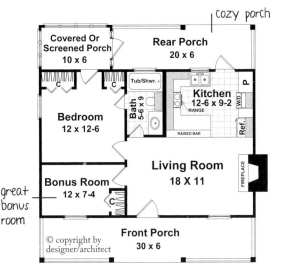

cozy porch

Covered Or Screened Porch
10 x 6

Rear Porch
20 x 6

Tub/Shwr.

Bath
5-6 x 9

Kitchen
12-6 x 9-2

RANGE

W/D

P

Ref.

Bedroom
12 x 12-6

RAISED BAR

Living Room
18 X 11

FIREPLACE

great bonus room

Bonus Room
12 x 7-4

C

© copyright by designer/architect

Front Porch
30 x 6

EDGEBRIAR CABIN

PLAN #C20-002D-7531

720 square feet of living area
width: 24'   depth: 30'
2 bedrooms, 1 bath
crawl space or slab foundation,
please specify when ordering
material list included

The Edgebriar cabin has an uncomplicated design that stands the test of time. Always a crowd pleaser, the deep covered front porch really creates the added outdoor space people crave. Whether reading in the shade or chatting with family and friends, this no doubt will be a favorite spot to unwind. The U-shaped kitchen is high function and overlooks the living area. Two bedrooms are placed in the back of the home near a laundry closet and full bathroom.

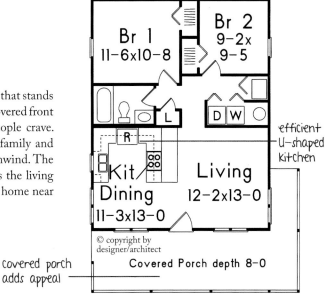

Br 1
11-6x10-8

Br 2
9-2x
9-5

efficient
U-shaped
kitchen

Kit/
Dining
11-3x13-0

Living
12-2x13-0

© copyright by
designer/architect

covered porch
adds appeal

Covered Porch depth 8-0

SAVANNA HILL CABIN

The Savanna Hill cabin has a coveted split bedroom layout for added privacy. The open kitchen/dining and great room are perfect for entertaining because the openness creates a more spacious feel. The laundry room is tucked off of the kitchen and hidden with a barn style door for added style. The rear porch is covered and 6' deep, which is ideal for expanding your living space outdoors when the weather is nice.

PLAN #C20-028D-0115

1035 square feet of living area
width: 44'   depth: 36'-6"
3 bedrooms, 2 baths
2" x 6" exterior walls
floating slab foundation standard;
monolithic slab, crawl space, basement or
walk-out basement available for a fee

BEDROOM 3
12-0 X 11-0

6' DEEP COVERED
PORCH

LAUNDRY
5-4 X 5-6

MASTER
BATH
8-8 X 9-6

BATH 2

KITCHEN/DINING
15-8 X 9-6

CLO.

BEDROOM 2
12-0 X 11-0

GREAT ROOM
15-8 X 12-0

MASTER
BEDROOM
14-0 X 12-0

© copyright by
designer/architect

6' DEEP COVERED
PORCH

covered porches
front and back

popular split
bedroom floor plan

ROVER CREEK CABIN

PLAN #C20-011D-0683

944 square feet of living area
width: 17'   depth: 41'
2 bedrooms, 1½ baths
2" x 6" exterior walls
crawl space or slab standard;
basement available for a fee

The Rover Creek cabin has been designed with a Modern Farmhouse flair that's currently so popular. The living/dining area has a large box-bay window for added architectural interest the homeowners will certainly appreciate. The kitchen has uncompromisable style and merges into the main gathering space. Upstairs, you'll find two bedrooms with a shared bath plus a handy washer and dryer closet right in the hall. Efficient and insanely stylish is a rare find!

© copyright by
designer/architect

first floor
489 sq. ft.

enough
space for
a rocking
chair

second floor
455 sq. ft.

super convenient
second floor
laundry closet

SCENIC HILL
Take time out at the Scenic Hill cabin and enjoy a covered front porch for story-telling at night as well as a vaulted open interior. The kitchen will be a hub of activity with its eating bar. Twin bedrooms provide a place to rest your head, and both have a closet.

PLAN #C20-141D-0218
1000 square feet of living area
width: 36'-6" depth: 34'
2 bedrooms, 1 bath
crawl space or slab foundation,
please specify when ordering

BOWMAN
The Bowman country cabin has a cathedral ceiling adding spaciousness, and a stone fireplace creating warmth. A large dining room extends off the kitchen and remains open. The master bedroom is tucked away by the kitchen for privacy.

PLAN #C20-020D-0015
1191 square feet of living area
width: 44'-6" depth: 59'
3 bedrooms, 2 baths
2" x 6" exterior walls
slab foundation standard;
basement or crawl space available for a fee

SHALLOWCOVE
The Shallowcove modern cabin is bound to be your all-time favorite place on earth. The kitchen/living area takes in waterfront views through a tall window wall that's the focal point.

PLAN #C20-126D-0993
572 square feet of living area
width: 22' depth: 26'
2 bedrooms, 1 bath
2" x 6" exterior walls
pilings foundation

GLEN ALLEN LANE
The Glen Allen Lane is a Craftsman delight with all architectural details from a century ago. The vaulted and beamed interior spaces add personality and create an inviting interior.

PLAN #C20-163D-0021
1164 square feet of living area
width: 79'-6" depth: 47'
2 bedrooms, 2 baths
2" x 6" exterior walls
slab foundation

SONA PIER
The Sona Pier cabin has a two-story corner window wall that is definitely meant to be admired. Vaulted tall ceilings, and a see-through fireplace shared by the living area and bedroom make this Modern style cabin definitely a head above the rest.

PLAN #C20-126D-1004
813 square feet of living area
width: 30' depth: 30'
1 bedroom, 1 bath
2" x 6" exterior walls
basement foundation

SOUTHDALE
The Southdale has the country charm you've always wanted in a small home. The deep covered porch will bring a smile to your face as you enter the open floor plan. Three bedrooms and two complete this ideal home.

PLAN #C20-170D-0035
1176 square feet of living area
width: 28' depth: 48'-6"
3 bedrooms, 2 baths
crawl space standard;
slab or monolithic slab, please specify when ordering

Blueprint PRICING and ORDERING + VISIT houseplansandmore.com + 1-800-373-2646

CARLO
The Carlo Modern cabin promises efficiency and cutting-edge style. A covered porch provides a place to rest; the inside is open space with a kitchen. A space-saving pocket door creates privacy for the bedroom.

PLAN #C20-126D-1148
396 square feet of living area
width: 22' depth: 18'
1 bedroom, 1 bath
2" x 6" exterior walls
pilings foundation

EVERETT CREEK
The Everett Creek Country cabin is ideal for a narrow lot. The open family room features a fireplace that radiates warmth into the nearby kitchen/breakfast area.

PLAN #C20-058D-0198
1061 square feet of living area
width: 28' depth: 52'
2 bedrooms, 2 baths
crawl space foundation

HARMONY BLUFF
The Harmony Bluff rustic cabin is topped with a soaring vaulted ceiling. The kitchen looks out over the great room with fireplace, and twin bedrooms provide comfort and privacy.

PLAN #C20-141D-0077
1000 square feet of living area
width: 27'   depth: 46'
2 bedrooms, 1 bath
slab foundation standard; crawl space, basement, or walk-out basement available for a fee

DILLON
Don't let this tiny modern cabin fool you, the Dillon cabin feels spacious with its slanted ceiling inside creating added space. Walk into a living area with the kitchen around the corner. The two bedrooms are on opposite sides for added privacy.

PLAN #C20-126D-1149
528 square feet of living area
width: 24'   depth: 22'
2 bedrooms, 1 bath
2" x 6" exterior walls
pilings foundation

MIKA
Whether the Mika modern cabin is built as an in-law suite, or as a stylish retreat, you will love that every inch is maximized for comfort. Front and back covered porches are great additions to the open interior layout.

PLAN #C20-126D-1152
599 square feet of living area
width: 38'   depth: 18'
1 bedroom, 1 bath
2" x 6" exterior walls
pier foundation

HILLTOP GREEN
The Hilltop Green cabin has one-of-a-kind modern style. A spiral staircase ascends to a loft overlooking the vaulted great room. The kitchen has a built-in eating bar with great room views.

PLAN #C20-080D-0015
840 square feet of living area
width: 20'   depth: 28'
1 bedroom, 1 bath
2" x 6" exterior walls
walk-out basement or basement foundation, please specify when ordering

APRIL KNOLL
This cozy cabin offers many comforts of home, including a vaulted great room, washer and dryer closet, and a U-shaped kitchen that opens onto the rear screened porch. Accessible via a ladder is a vaulted loft that overlooks the great room.

PLAN #C20-077D-0286
1016 square feet of living area
width: 30' depth: 36'
2 bedrooms, 1 bath
crawl space foundation standard;
slab available for a fee

RUSTY RIDGE
The open floor plan is fantastic in the Rusty Ridge Craftsman style home. The foyer includes plenty of closet space. The washer and dryer are located on the first floor, and the second floor consists of two bedrooms with large closets plus a full bathroom.

PLAN #C20-032D-0808
900 square feet of living area
width: 32' depth: 24'
2 bedrooms, 1¹/₂ baths
2" x 6" exterior walls
basement foundation standard; crawl space, floating slab, or monolithic slab available for a fee

CALRIVER
The Calriver country cabin boasts an open floor plan and pure comfort for the homeowner. The kitchen/breakfast room is entirely open to the cozy sitting area with a fireplace.

PLAN #C20-058D-0197
781 square feet of living area
width: 35' depth: 30'-8"
1 bedroom, 1 bath
crawl space foundation

LONG MEADOW
This country cabin would be a great in-law suite with its large bathroom with utility room and walk-in shower. A living room, nearby kitchen, and master bedroom complete the home.

PLAN #C20-141D-0230
676 square feet of living area
width: 26' depth: 32'
1 bedroom, 1 bath
slab or crawl space standard;
basement or daylight basement available for a fee

LIVING LARGE IN A SMALL HOME

Out with the old and in with the new. Gone are the days of excessively large and wasteful mansions. Now, small homes rule the market. They cost less to maintain, they are easier to clean, they bring family closer together, and the taxes are far lower.

With so many benefits, it's no wonder that many families are making the switch to more modestly sized abodes. However, it's important to remember the cost — less space! This means that you must maintain optimal use of your available space, clear out the clutter, and plan out everything. No more impulse buys because they simply won't fit into your smaller place!

FLOOR PLAN

Consider every room carefully and evaluate your needs. For the smaller home, an open floor plan with fewer interior walls opens up your available space and creates the illusion of even more space since pesky walls aren't obstructing the view. High ceilings also open up the home for relatively low cost and they help reduce feelings of claustrophobia and restriction. Additionally, certain rooms such as formal dining and living rooms have outlived their usefulness. Only utilized a handful of times a year, converting these outdated rooms into multipurpose spaces or offices is certainly a viable option.

DOORS AND WINDOWS

Doors are another feature to consider in your small home. With limited space, every little bit counts, and installing trendy barn-style or pocket doors instead of hinge doors can free up an average of 10 square feet. That's a lot of space that you can put to good use!

Other ways to create the impression of space include adding large windows into your design or even a skylight. These windows filter in more natural light, brightening and reinforcing the feeling of spaciousness in the interior.

STORAGE

Once you have the floor plan figured out, it's time to think about a very important matter: storage. Over our lifetimes we accumulate stuff. Whether it's useful or full of memories, we need places to put our knickknacks, and with less space, organization and creativity play key roles. However, no matter how organized you are, if there is no room, there is simply no room.

So if you're downsizing, or trying to get your smaller home in order, remember that you may need to assess all of your belongings before picking nonessentials to throw out.

Now that you're left with essentials and anything that you can't bear to part with, it's time to consider alternative storage options. Built-in shelves, for example, free up a lot of floor space and create a more open atmosphere. Also, wall hooks, floor-to-ceiling shelving, and storage under the stairs or bed can clean up the disorder of everyday life. It is important to remember that open shelving, as opposed to closed cabinets, creates a more open feel and the illusion of more space. And, don't forget to utilize your full vertical storage capacity! Oftentimes we neglect to fill up the available vertical space and just try to cram everything in at eye level or below. You may need to keep a footstool nearby, but the added storage space is well worth it.

COLOR

When you're painting your small house, just remember that dark colors create an intimate, cozy feeling whereas lighter hues open up a room. So, depending upon how you want to feel, you may want a nice and cozy, darker home, or you may want an open and fresh, lighter home. You may even want a mix of dark and light rooms. In creating an effective light color scheme, it is important to choose pale, soft paint colors for your walls and then use your furniture to create the colored accents. Stick to plain solid colored furniture because it will keep your small room from looking cluttered by bold prints and patterns.

DECORATION AND FURNITURE

It's time to decorate your home, but you don't want to waste space on flashy, useless decorations. Instead, keep the displayed knickknacks to a minimum to reduce the visual clutter and give a more airy feel to your home. Without all of the odds and ends closing in on your visual field, you're free to appreciate the items that are on display without feeling crowded out. Also, hanging mirrors on your walls will give the illusion of more space and provide an attractive wall embellishment at the same time.

Furnishing your small space can be both exciting and challenging. Not everything will fit well, so remember to plan out your furniture. Instead of choosing a myriad of smaller furnishings, pick out several larger pieces to create a focal point in the room and avoid the muddled, chaotic feel of too much small furniture. Also, be sure to consider the multi-purpose potential of your furniture. Ottomans and chests can double as storage or coffee tables. Let your creativity reign and you will give your house a unique, yet functional interior perfect for living large in a small home!

COTTAGES

Plan #C20-032D-0358 is found on page 71.

While cabins evoke a sense of all things rustic, cottages shift toward a charming, nostalgic country feel. Like their rustic counterpart, cottages are small in size, but packed with personality. Cottages steer clear of a cabin's usually rustic exterior and are often adorned with pastel colors and intricate trim work that borderlines Victorian style. Cottages are especially popular near the water, both coastal and lakeside, and can create the ideal getaway home or investment property. Whatever your specific need, you will fall in love with the undeniable charm these cottages provide.

ROBBIN COTTAGE

Live life like a fairytale in the European-inspired, quaint Robbin cottage. With attention to detail at every turn, cottage life is definitely not primitive in this luxurious cottage that boasts an amenity-packed kitchen, an open floor plan, vaulted living area, and homeowner quarters that are comfortable and bright. Don't let size fool you; this cottage is designed to pamper and provides a luxury environment to prove it.

© copyright by designer/architect

VAULTED
MASTER
14/2 X 10/8 +/-

BLT-IN

VAULTED
BR. 2
10/8 X 11/2

W/D

BLT-IN PAN

large coat closet and pantry combo

washer and dryer space in the bathroom

PORCH

VAULTED
LIVING
12/0 X 15/8 +

(8' CLG)

PLAN #C20-011D-0313

782 square feet of living area
width: 24'   depth: 44'
2 bedrooms, 1 bath
2" x 6" exterior walls
crawl space or slab foundation standard;
basement available for a fee

SAN FERNANDO COTTAGE

The San Fernando cottage has a Modern Farmhouse bungalow feel and a covered metal awning overhang above the front porch creating excellent curb appeal. Enter through the double French doors and discover a mud room style entry so popular today with a coat closet on the left, and a built-in bench with hooks above on the right. Just drop your things and head right on in! The great room, dining space and kitchen are designed to enjoy plenty of sunshine from multiple windows. Inside and out, this cottage is a star!

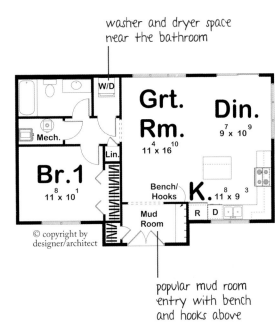

washer and dryer space near the bathroom

W/D

Grt. Rm. 11 x 16 ⁴ ¹⁰

Din. 9 x 10 ⁷ ⁹

Mech.

Lin.

Br.1 11 x 10 ⁸ ¹

Bench/ Hooks

K. 11 x 9 ⁸ ³

Mud Room

R   D

© copyright by designer/architect

popular mud room entry with bench and hooks above

PLAN #C20-123D-0263

756 square feet of living area
width: 36'   depth: 23'
1 bedroom, 1 bath
slab foundation standard;
crawl space, basement, or
walk-out basement available for a fee

BELLE COVE COTTAGE

Elegantly European, the Belle Cove cottage mimics the style of a French Chateau, but on a much smaller scale. This design perfects the open layout without a hitch. Two bedrooms, each with their own bath, create privacy and everyday comfort for guests or a live-in parent. The central hub is the kitchen where all activity will radiate from. Dining and living areas effectively merge, forming a larger area. And there's even a one-car garage.

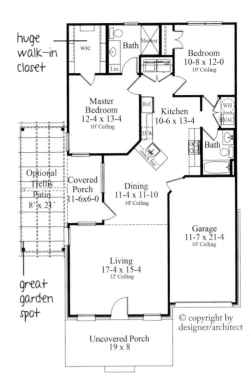

huge
walk-in
closet

wic — Bath — Lin. — Shower

Bedroom
10-8 x 12-0
10' Ceiling

Master
Bedroom
12-4 x 13-4
10' Ceiling

Ref.

Kitchen
10-6 x 13-4

WH
HVAC

D W

Bath

Snack Bar

Optional
Trellis
Patio
8' x 22'

Covered
Porch
11-6x6-0

Dining
11-4 x 11-10
10' Ceiling

Garage
11-7 x 21-4
10' Ceiling

great
garden
spot

Living
17-4 x 15-4
12' Ceiling

© copyright by
designer/architect

Uncovered Porch
19 x 8

PLAN #C20-084D-0052

1170 square feet of living area
width: 38'-6"   depth: 48'-6"
2 bedrooms, 2 baths
slab foundation standard;
crawl space or basement available for a fee

DIGBY COTTAGE

The Digby cottage is a fantasy come true! Have you ever seen such a stylish, quaint dwelling? Its rustic appeal and attention to detail begs you to knock on the door and invite yourself in. Designed as guest quarters, this cottage has a cozy corner fireplace for added ambiance. The kitchenette is efficient and offers basic amenities. A spacious walk-in closet provides more than ample storage. The bathroom has a walk-in shower, great for people of all ages and abilities. This cottage is what dreams are made of!

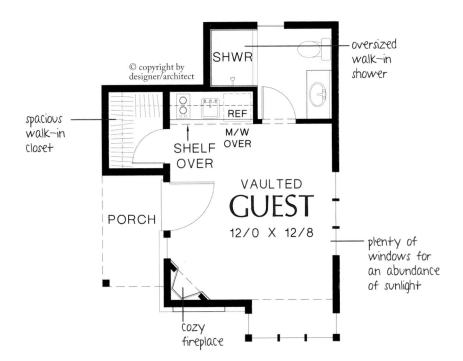

© copyright by designer/architect

SHWR

oversized walk-in shower

spacious walk-in closet

REF

M/W OVER

SHELF OVER

VAULTED
GUEST
12/0 X 12/8

PORCH

plenty of windows for an abundance of sunlight

cozy fireplace

PLAN #C20-011D-0431

300 square feet of living area
width: 17'-6"   depth: 23'
1 bedroom, 1 bath
2" x 6" exterior walls
slab foundation

MILFORD COVE COTTAGE

The Milford Cove cottage has an alluring Palladian-style window gracing its exterior, while it also floods the living room with added sunlight in the interior. The incredible dining room flows into a kitchen that offers a dual sink, handsome cabinetry, and loads of counterspace. The master suite is simply luxurious with bright windows, a walk-in closet, and a separate shower for the ultimate in relaxation. The second floor has two bedrooms and a full bath, which can easily accommodate a family.

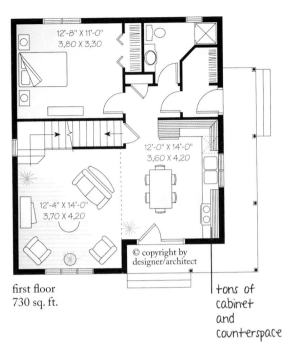

12'-8" X 11'-0"
3,80 X 3,30

12'-0" X 14'-0"
3,60 X 4,20

12'-4" X 14'-0"
3,70 X 4,20

© copyright by
designer/architect

first floor
730 sq. ft.

tons of
cabinet
and
counterspace

14'-4" X 11'-0"
4,30 X 3,30

10'-10" X 11'-0"
3,25 X 3,30

second floor
438 sq. ft.

loft–style
bedroom

PLAN #C20-032D-0554

1168 square feet of living area
width: 25'-8"   depth: 30'
3 bedrooms, 2 baths
2" x 6" exterior walls
basement foundation standard;
crawl space, monolithic slab,
or floating slab available for a fee

HAYWARD LANE COTTAGE

The Hayward Lane cottage has that welcoming covered front porch big enough to sit and enjoy when it's too warm for direct sun on the patio. This one-story design embraces an open atmosphere on the first floor, making it a fun floor plan when entertaining. Plus, it has some famous extras like a roomy mud room with a bench and lockers and a separate laundry room that makes it a star for organization. With plenty of room to grow, this home has plenty of extra space on the lower level. Don't let the undeniable charm and comfort of the Hayward Lane cottage pass you by.

K.
15 x 14
10'-0" Ceiling

Pantry

Mbr.
12 x 13
10'-0" Ceiling

walk-in pantry and island in the kitchen

Din.
15 x 8
10'-0" Ceiling

Coffee Bar

R

Lin.

W D

DN

Mud Room

Liv.
14 x 12
10'-0" Ceiling

Bench/ Lockers

Covered Porch

Gar.
19 x 22

first floor
1030 sq. ft.

© copyright by
designer/architect

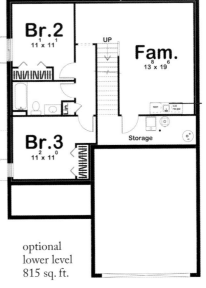

Br.2
11 x 11

UP

Fam.
13 x 19

fun entertaining area with wet bar

Lin.

Br.3
11 x 11

Storage

optional
lower level
815 sq. ft.

PLAN #C20-123D-0171

1030 square feet of living area
815 bonus square feet
width: 37'   depth: 49'
1 bedroom, 1¹/₂ baths
basement foundation standard;
crawl space, slab, or walk-out basement
available for a fee

LYNDALE COTTAGE

Simple yet beautiful Craftsman-style windows bring interest to the exterior of the cheerful Lyndale cottage. The comfortable covered front porch is the perfect place to sit back, enjoy the outdoors, and wave to the neighbors. The lovely kitchen is cozy yet highly functional. The romantic master suite is privately located on the second floor and contains a large window in the bedroom, as well as a private bathroom with a double-bowl vanity. Practical, functional, and graced with Craftsman style, this cottage is refreshing yet timeless at the same time.

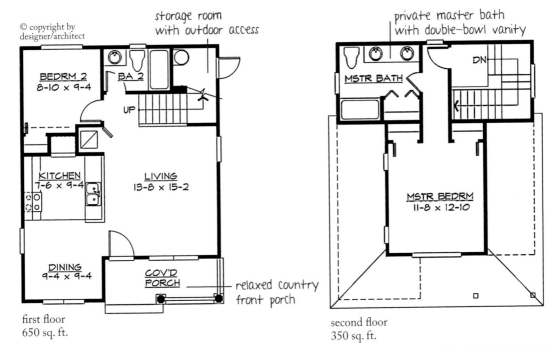

storage room
with outdoor access

private master bath
with double-bowl vanity

© copyright by
designer/architect

BEDRM 2
8-10 x 9-4

BA 2

UP

DN

MSTR BATH

KITCHEN
7-6 x 9-4

LIVING
13-8 x 15-2

MSTR BEDRM
11-8 x 12-10

DINING
9-4 x 9-4

COV'D
PORCH

relaxed country
front porch

first floor
650 sq. ft.

second floor
350 sq. ft.

PLAN #C20-071D-0013

1000 square feet of living area
width: 24'   depth: 30'
2 bedrooms, 2 baths
2" x 6" exterior walls
crawl space foundation

FAIR VIEW COTTAGE

The Fair View cottage offers all of the things cottage living is about. Abundant charm, Southern-style covered front and side porches, and a welcoming floor plan. The family room with fireplace greets all those who come through the front door. A bay-shaped kitchen with island is ready for any task at hand and can easily reach a grill on the deck. Life's simple pleasures will be enjoyed to the fullest in this darling home.

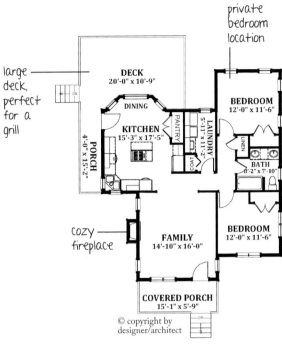

large deck, perfect for a grill

private bedroom location

DECK 20'-0" x 10'-9"

DINING

KITCHEN 15'-3" x 17'-5"

PORCH 4'-0" x 15'-2"

PANTRY

LAUNDRY 5'-11" x 11'-2"

COAT

COAT

BEDROOM 12'-0" x 11'-6"

LINEN

BATH 8'-2" x 7'-10"

cozy fireplace

FAMILY 14'-10" x 16'-0"

BEDROOM 12'-0" x 11'-6"

COVERED PORCH 15'-1" x 5'-9"

© copyright by designer/architect

PLAN #C20-139D-0001

1068 square feet of living area
width: 39'-7"   depth: 51'-9"
2 bedrooms, 1 bath
2" x 6" exterior walls
crawl space foundation standard;
slab, basement, daylight basement or
walk-out basement available for a fee

FAIRHAVEN HILL COTTAGE

Life in the Fairhaven Hill cottage will be bliss! Besides its abundance of exterior charm, this tiny home has the most cheerful interior. Walls of windows emit tons of natural sunlight, creating an interior you'll be excited to decorate. An expansive L-shaped kitchen flows seamlessly into the living area. The bedroom has direct access into the bathroom. Whether this is a vacation cottage or a permanent dwelling, this cottage is truly something special.

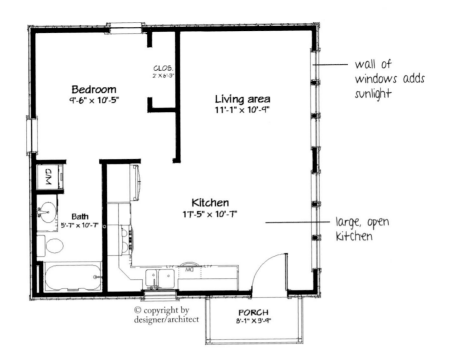

Bedroom
9'-6" × 10'-5"

CLOS.
2' × 6'-3"

Living area
11'-1" × 10'-9"

wall of
windows adds
sunlight

Bath
5'-7" × 10'-7"

Kitchen
17'-5" × 10'-7"

large, open
kitchen

© copyright by
designer/architect

PORCH
8'-1" × 3'-9"

PLAN #C20-156D-0007

528 square feet of living area
width: 24'   depth: 26'
1 bedroom, 1 bath
slab foundation standard;
crawl space available for a fee

DRIFT TIDE COTTAGE

Spacious and open, the Drift Tide's interior feels much larger than its true size thanks to the absence of walls between the spaces, while its exterior is fashioned after the popular Modern Farmhouse style. The kitchen features a sizable island with seating for up to four people. Two symmetrical bedrooms and baths comprise the rear of the home and offer equal amenities. The laundry room has a handy sink and outdoor access. The great room/dining area extends off the kitchen and offers a quality open living concept.

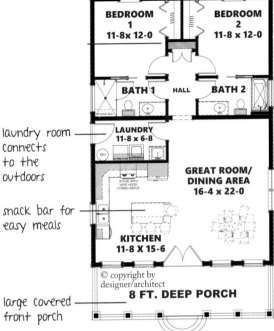

BEDROOM 1
11-8x 12-0

BEDROOM 2
11-8 x 12-0

BATH 1   HALL   BATH 2

laundry room connects to the outdoors

LAUNDRY
11-8 x 6-8

WH

STOVE WITH VENT HOOD COMBO ABOVE

GREAT ROOM/ DINING AREA
16-4 x 22-0

snack bar for easy meals

KITCHEN
11-8 X 15-6

© copyright by designer/architect

large covered front porch

8 FT. DEEP PORCH

PLAN #C20-028D-0116

1120 square feet of living area
width: 28'   depth: 48'
2 bedrooms, 2 baths
2" x 6" exterior walls
slab foundation

CANTON CREST COTTAGE

The Canton Crest cottage has covered front and rear porches with ceiling fans, keeping you comfortable in balmy weather. A dramatic vaulted ceiling crowns the family room and kitchen, creating a truly effective openness. Two generously sized bedrooms, each with a walk-in closet, share a bathroom.

PLAN #C20-013D-0154

953 square feet of living area
width: 36'   depth: 42'-4"
2 bedrooms, 1½ baths
crawl space foundation standard;
basement or slab available for a fee

both bedrooms have
direct access to the bathroom

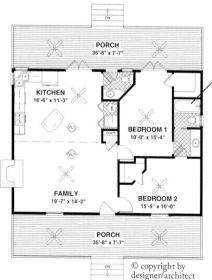

© copyright by
designer/architect

SUMMERLEDGE COTTAGE

PLAN #C20-007D-0128

1072 square feet of living area
345 bonus square feet
width: 52'   depth: 40'-8"
2 bedrooms, 2 baths
walk-out basement foundation

The Summerledge cottage integrates open and screened front porches, guaranteeing comfortable summer enjoyment. An oversized garage includes a shop and storage. The U-shaped kitchen and breakfast area are adjacent to a vaulted living room with patio access through sliding glass doors. Optional living space, including a third bedroom and a bath, can be found on the lower level.

flexibility to increase square footage

Br 3 13-4x12-3

Basement

optional lower level 345 sq. ft.

Basement

MBr 11-7x15-6

Br 2 10-0x12-11

Hall

Shop

Garage 21-8x26-4

© copyright by designer/architect

Patio

Hall

Kit 9-7x9-0

Living 14-0x18-9

Brk fst 10-9x9-0

Screened Porch 18-4x13-0

first floor 1072 sq. ft.

Porch

breezy screened porch for outdoor enjoyment

DANBURY HOLLOW COTTAGE

The Danbury Hollow cottage has a refined cottage feel that just oozes charm. It is also the perfect size for a small or narrow lot. The angled kitchen is intriguing to the eye and contains lots of counter space for easily prepping daily meals. One open living space creates an enjoyable environment for entertaining or relaxation. Two sizable bedrooms skillfully share a bath with a large whirlpool tub.

PLAN #C20-032D-0116

946 square feet of living area
width: 30'   depth: 35'
2 bedrooms, 1 bath
2" x 6" exterior walls
basement foundation standard;
crawl space, monolithic slab,
or floating slab available for a fee

18'-0" X 12'-0"
5,40 X 3,60

10'-4" X 9'-6"
3,10 X 2,85

open floor plan

13'-0" X 15'-0"
3,90 X 4,50

13'-0" X 11'-0"
3,90 X 3,30

© copyright by
designer/architect

WILDBROOK COTTAGE

PLAN #C20-032D-0358

1148 square feet of living area
width: 28'   depth: 26'
1 bedroom, 1½ baths
2" x 6" exterior walls
basement foundation standard;
crawl space, monolithic slab,
floating slab available for a fee

The Wildbrook cottage is completely open for a bright, cheerful atmosphere. The kitchen includes a unique island with seating for quick meals, or space to serve buffet-style. The half bath on the first floor has space for a washer and dryer. French doors lead to the majestic second floor master bedroom that enjoys a huge walk-in closet and a private bath with a separate whirlpool tub and corner shower.

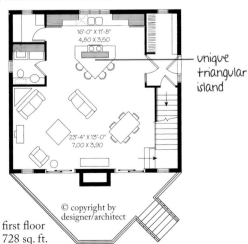

16'-0" X 11'-8"
4,80 X 3,50

unique triangular island

23'-4" X 13'-0"
7,00 X 3,90

© copyright by designer/architect

first floor
728 sq. ft.

massive bedroom and closet

16'-0" x 11'-2"
4,80 X 3,35

second floor
420 sq. ft.

spacious two-story ceiling

HAVERHILL COTTAGE

The vaulted ceiling in the family room of the Haverhill cottage will create quite a stir. The covered entry porch provides plenty of shade on warm, summer evenings. The open L-shaped kitchen has a functional layout. The convenient laundry room is located near the rear entry and bedroom #1. Bedroom #2 on the second floor is a great space for a home office or guest room.

PLAN #C20-040D-0028

828 square feet of living area
width: 28'   depth: 31'-6"
2 bedrooms, 1 bath
crawl space foundation

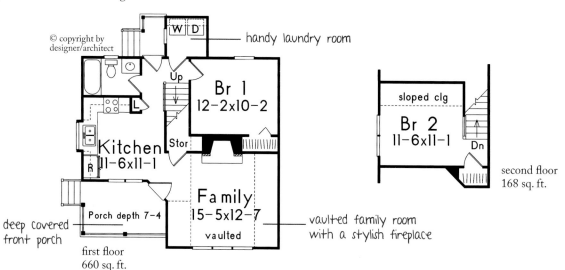

© copyright by
designer/architect

handy laundry room

W D

Up

Br 1
12-2x10-2

Kitchen
11-6x11-1

Stor

R

deep covered
front porch

Porch depth 7-4

Family
15-5x12-7

vaulted

first floor
660 sq. ft.

sloped clg

Br 2
11-6x11-1

Dn

second floor
168 sq. ft.

vaulted family room
with a stylish fireplace

SUMMERSMILL COTTAGE

PLAN #C20-007D-0135

801 square feet of living area
width: 57'   depth: 36'-4"
2 bedrooms, 1 bath
slab foundation

A wraparound porch, roof dormer, and fancy stonework all contribute to the delightful and charming exterior of the Summersmill cottage. A vaulted living room enjoys a stone fireplace and lots of windows. The well-equipped kitchen has a snack bar and bayed dining area with access to a rear patio. Two bedrooms with a bath and a large workshop in the garage for the family handyman are great extras in this small floor plan.

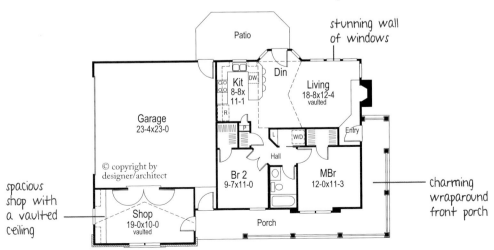

AVONDALE LANE COTTAGE

The Avondale Lane cottage has a friendly, welcoming feel the minute you lay your eyes on it. Its charming covered porch will put a smile on your face. Inside, the vaulted living room remains separate from the kitchen with enough space for dining. The bedroom is generous in size and has two closets for keeping things tidy. A roomy bath is in a convenient location. Living is easy in this lovely little cottage.

PLAN #C20-156D-0006

550 square feet of living area
width: 25'   depth: 28'
1 bedroom, 1 bath
slab foundation standard;
crawl space available for a fee

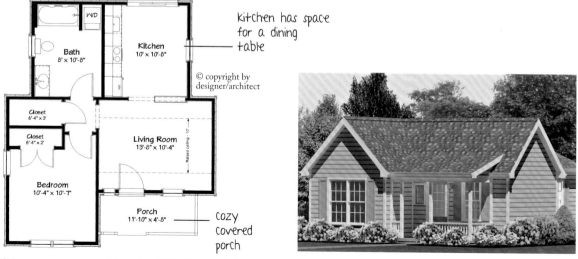

Bath
8' x 10'-8"

Kitchen
10' x 10'-8"

kitchen has space for a dining table

© copyright by designer/architect

Closet
6'-4" x 3'

Closet
6'-4" x 2'

Living Room
13'-8" x 10'-4"

Bedroom
10'-4" x 10'-7"

Porch
11'-10" x 4'-8"

cozy covered porch

FOXLAND COTTAGE

PLAN #C20-045D-0017

954 square feet of living area
width: 25'-8"   depth: 30'
3 bedrooms, 2 baths
basement foundation

Step from the shaded covered front porch inside this charming cottage and find a convenient coat closet near the front entry. The kitchen has a cozy bayed eating area. The great room has access to both the front and back porches. The master bedroom has a walk-in closet and a private bath. The second floor is comprised of two bedrooms and a full bath centered between them for convenience. Charm and function are equally achieved in this friendly cottage!

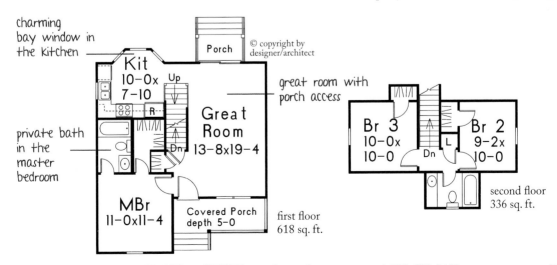

charming bay window in the kitchen

© copyright by designer/architect

Porch

Kit
10-0x
7-10

Up

R

great room with porch access

Great Room
13-8x19-4

Dn

private bath in the master bedroom

MBr
11-0x11-4

Covered Porch
depth 5-0

first floor
618 sq. ft.

Br 3
10-0x
10-0

Dn

L

Br 2
9-2x
10-0

second floor
336 sq. ft.

SHAKER LANE COTTAGE

Timeless Colonial charm has been perfected in the Shaker Lane cottage. Covered front and back porches truly make this home, while spilling living into the outdoors in a seamless way. The great room has a fireplace as a focal point and the bedroom and bath have a nearby washer and dryer closet.

PLAN #C20-011D-0316

960 square feet of living area
width: 30'   depth: 48'
1 bedroom, 1 bath
2" x 6" exterior walls
crawl space or slab foundation standard;
basement available for a fee

© copyright by
designer/architect

large front
and rear porches

PORCH
26/0 X 8/0

11/0 X 9/0
(9' CLG.)

REF PAN

W/D

GREAT RM.
16/8 X 23/8
(9' CLG.)

LIN

BR.
11/0 X 13/0
(9' CLG.)

SHLVS

BUILT-IN
GUEST BED

unique
built-in
guest bed
behind
barn-style
doors

PORCH
26/0 X 8/0

OLSON LANE COTTAGE

PLAN #C20-051D-0847

1047 square feet of living area
width: 40'   depth: 46'
2 bedrooms, 1 bath
2" x 6" exterior walls
basement foundation standard;
crawl space or slab available for a fee

The Olson Lane Craftsman cottage has tremendous curb appeal with its spacious covered front porch offering additional outdoor living space. The open-concept floor plan has the kitchen, dining, and great room blended together, creating a more spacious living area. The bedrooms are located to the left of the home behind the garage for privacy.

open vaulted living space

DECK

MBR.
9'-1 1/8" CEILING
15'8"x13'0"

KIT.
VAULTED CEILING
9'0"x9'6"

DIN. RM.
VAULTED CEILING
8'6"x9'6"

BR. #2
9'-1 1/8" CEILING
11'8"x10'6"

GRT. RM.
VAULTED CEILING
17'6"x14'6"

E.
CATHEDRAL CEILING

2 CAR GARAGE
20'4"x20'8"

© copyright by designer/architect

high ceiling for openness

NORDIKA
The Nordika cottage has an upscale kitchen with an island with space for five people and a walk-in pantry. Two bedrooms and a posh bath with a spa tub and a separate shower make this home very comfortable despite its smaller size.

PLAN #C20-032D-1155
1140 square feet of living area
1140 bonus square feet
width: 52' depth: 32'
2 bedrooms, 1 bath
basement foundation standard; crawl space, monolithic slab or floating slab available for a fee

MILLER LANE
The Miller Lane cottage transports you to the Lowcountry and begs you to invite neighbors for a crawfish boil. Two covered porches provide a great outdoor escape. The great room has a gas fireplace for chilly nights.

PLAN #C20-028D-0108
890 square feet of living area
width: 33' depth: 40'
2 bedrooms, 1 bath
floating slab foundation standard; monolithic slab, crawl space, basement or walk-out basement for a fee

GROVEVILLE
An open kitchen and two sizable bedrooms complete the stylish and sensible Groveville cottage design. The open layout makes it feels larger than its actual size.

PLAN #C20-130D-0403
788 square feet of living area
width: 24' depth: 36'
2 bedrooms, 1 bath
slab foundation standard; crawl space or basement available for a fee

AVONELLE
The adorable Avonelle compact home offers great energy efficiency. One wall of the living space was designed to accommodate a Murphy bed and front and rear porches add additional outdoor living space..

PLAN #C20-020D-0404
523 square feet of living area
width: 26' depth: 42'
1 bedroom, 1 bath
2" x 6" exterior walls
crawl space foundation standard; slab available for a fee

ROSEPORT
This is the perfect home with a timeless exterior and a charming front porch. The Roseport's living room is open to the kitchen, while the bayed breakfast area adjoins the kitchen via a pass-through snack bar. The roomy bedrooms also have walk-in closets.

PLAN #C20-007D-0109
888 square feet of living area
width: 35' depth: 38'
2 bedrooms, 1 bath
basement foundation;
crawl space or slab available for a fee

AUBREY
Step into the Aubrey compact cottage from the inviting covered porch and discover a pleasant great room with enough space for entertaining. The spacious kitchen/dining area is just steps away and offers a functional layout for comfortable cooking and dining.

PLAN #C20-121D-0033
944 square feet of living area
width: 32' depth: 34'
2 bedrooms, 1 bath
basement standard;
crawl space or slab available for a fee

BLAYLOCK
The Blaylock cottage is ideal for someone wanting just enough space. Easy to maintain and efficiently designed, this cottage also has an optional lower level with an in-law apartment and outdoor access.

PLAN #C20-172D-0020
943 square feet of living area
931 bonus square feet
width: 61' depth: 25'-6"
2 bedrooms, 1 bath
basement foundation standard; crawl space, slab, daylight basement or walk-out basement for a fee

BRIARIDGE
The Briaridge cottage enjoys shady porches for relaxing evenings. The living room and dining area are open to an L-shaped kitchen. The bedroom has a full bath, walk-in closet, and rear porch access.

PLAN #C20-007D-0199
496 square feet of living area
width: 39' depth: 33'
1 bedroom, 1 bath
slab foundation

SPRINGDALE

A stylish cottage retreat, the Springdale cottage has a delightful country porch, perfect for quiet evenings. The living room offers an arched front feature window inviting the sun indoors and includes a fireplace, dining area, and private patio access.

PLAN #C20-007D-0105

1084 square feet of living area
width: 35'   depth: 40'-8"
2 bedrooms, 2 baths
basement foundation standard;
crawl space or slab available for a fee

BRANSON BLUFF

The perfect country retreat, the Branson Bluff features a vaulted entry and a living room with skylights and a plant shelf. The kitchen has plenty of storage and a breakfast bar. Double-doors lead to a vaulted bedroom with bath access.

PLAN #C20-007D-0029

576 square feet of living area
width: 24'   depth: 30'
1 bedroom, 1 bath
crawl space foundation standard;
slab available for a fee

COTSWOLD

This cottage's charm is achieved thanks to gables, decorative trim, Old English windows, a balcony, and flower boxes. Inside the Cotswold, find a living area with a cozy wood-burning fireplace.

PLAN #C20-007D-0217

1075 square feet of living area
width: 38'   depth: 34'
1 bedroom, 1 bath
crawl space foundation

VALENCIA BAY

The Valencia Bay cottage enjoys a kitchen island overlooking the great room with fireplace. The bedroom has a walk-in closet and a full-size laundry room is a memorable feature.

PLAN #C20-123D-0264

733 square feet of living area
width: 34'-8"   depth: 32'
1 bedroom, 1 bath
slab foundation standard; crawl space, basement or walk-out basement available for a fee

ROLLINS
The Rollins cottage has so many great features including a two-story living room with clerestory windows above, a breakfast bar for three people plus a nearby dinette, a study alcove under the stairs, a laundry room, and a private second floor bedroom.

PLAN #C20-130D-0363
597 square feet of living area
width: 16' depth: 29'
1 bedroom, 1 bath
slab foundation standard;
basement or crawl space available for a fee

BERRYBRIDGE
The covered front porch of the Berrybridge cottage will see many days and nights of summer enjoyment. Step into the living room with a fireplace and a nearby kitchen with a door to the yard. The bedrooms are private with lots of closet space.

PLAN #C20-008D-0159
733 square feet of living area
width: 30' depth: 32'
2 bedrooms, 1 bath
pier foundation

OAK COVE
The Oak Cove cottage is outfitted with a covered porch, creating a place to relax in nature. The family room is warmed by a fireplace, while the kitchen has a pantry and the bath has washer/dryer space.

PLAN #C20-040D-0029
1028 square feet of living area
width: 30' depth: 30'-6"
3 bedrooms, 1 bath
crawl space foundation

GATEHILL
The Gatehill cottage has vaulted ceilings in the sitting area and bedroom making it feel larger than its true size. A unique cellar below the home offers a great storm safety space.

PLAN #C20-058D-0202
740 square feet of living area
width: 30'4" depth: 42'-4"
1 bedroom, 1 bath
crawl space foundation

VACATION HOME MAINTENANCE

If you're lucky enough to own a vacation home, then you probably long for the moment when you can escape your daily routine and head to this special place. Vacation homes provide a mental escape located in a tranquil place away from the errands, carpooling, and all of the headaches associated with running a household every day. Whether you have a cabin on the lake or a beach front cottage, being only a temporary resident can pose some special problems and maintenance issues for a homeowner. Here are some important things to remember when trying to maintain a home while you are away.

SECURITY

It can be a difficult task keeping your home safe and secure when you're not there. Daily activity and the presence of those who dwell there are an automatic safeguard from theft and vandalism. The minute you leave, your precious home is at risk.

Here are a few easy and inexpensive ways to keep your home from looking vulnerable.

+ Add automatic lights that are on a timer or can be controlled remotely with an app from your smart phone. Having lights surrounding the exterior will make those who are interested in breaking in less comfortable about acting it out. Also, have interior lamps or lights to turn on regularly, which will keep up the appearance of constant activity. Have a kitchen lamp turn on early in the evening and possibly a bedroom lamp remain on later into the night.

+ If you have a friend that lives near your vacation home, have them occasionally drive by and survey the area. If they know your patterns and routines, they will be sure to notice if anything looks out of place almost immediately.

+ Even if the home is not used on a regular basis, it is still important to keep it maintained and clean so it is ready to be enjoyed the minute you arrive. Consider hiring a cleaning service to keep up your home in-between visits and protect the

interior from dust and mold. Plus, having routine visitors lets intruders know the home is well-kept and cared for by the owners.

+ Installing a security system is another way to ensure your favorite getaway is safe. Although there will be some costs involved with installation, typically the monthly or quarterly payments for the service are relatively inexpensive.

MAINTENANCE

Proper heating, cooling, and other maintenance measures need to be

considered even when the home is not in use. Not having the interior set on a proper temperature can cause damage to pipes, flooring, and other areas. Here are several maintenance ideas to keep your home welcoming when you arrive for a week of fun and relaxation.

HVAC – In the winter, the ideal temperature for keeping your home safe from frozen pipes is between 50 and 55 degrees. During the summer, be sure the interior does not become overheated. If your home gets too hot or too moist, mold and rust can occur.

Appliances – If you will not be visiting your vacation cabin or cottage for a while, consider unplugging appliances. Many fires have been attributed to everyday appliances with faulty wiring. Unplugging automatically eliminates this hazard.

Pests – Secure windows, patch up holes, and install mesh over attic vents and soffits to keep mice, squirrels, and birds out. Who wants to show up for a relaxing vacation and discover you'll be sharing it with these creatures? It's a lot easier to keep them out than it is to find a way to remove them once they're in.

Protect Outdoor Furniture – Cover outdoor furniture to reduce the possibility of storm damage. Shut down your gas grill to avoid leaks and chain it to a railing to keep it from blowing away during an intense storm. Securing everything outdoors will keep damage to your home's siding and windows at a minimum.

These special maintenance tips and ideas will make your visits to your special vacation getaway enjoyable and stress-free. Taking these simple steps before you leave will keep from unexpected disasters presenting themselves when you return the next time.

VACATION
HOMES

Plan #C20-126D-0992 is found on page 86.

Vacation homes come in a wide variety of styles, but these dwellings are often found in waterfront, coastal, or mountain locations, perfect for getting away from it all and taking a much needed break from reality. Many vacation-style homes are designed for carefree living, typically are smaller in size and feature efficient, open floor plans and plenty of large windows to easily enjoy surrounding views, and are designed for a sloping lot. With a diverse selection of styles and sizes, there is a vacation home waiting for everyone.

PLATEAU PEAK VACATION HOME

Plateau Peak is a rugged modern mountain escape offering a private getaway ideal for views of all kinds. With windows everywhere, this rustic cabin proves that no angle is out of sight. Step in from the covered porch and find a main gathering space with a kitchen on one wall, allowing the cabin to remain entirely open. The bedroom is steps away and has a full bath outside its doors. When life takes over, grab a bag and head here to completely recharge from the daily grind.

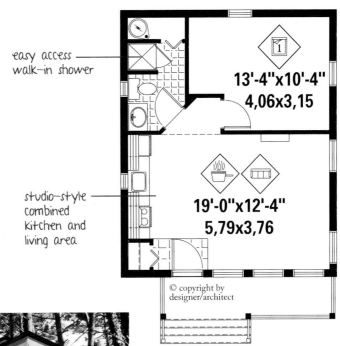

easy access walk-in shower

13'-4"x10'-4"
4,06x3,15

studio-style combined kitchen and living area

19'-0"x12'-4"
5,79x3,76

PLAN #C20-126D-0992

480 square feet of living area
width: 20'   depth: 24'
1 bedroom, 1 bath
2" x 6" exterior walls
crawl space foundation

PAULINE VACATION HOME

Step onto this charming front porch that is sure to open into a home just as charming. The family room, dining area, and kitchen transition seamlessly into one another for an open and spacious interior design. There is plenty of storage in this home with many closets and pantries. The master bedroom has a generous closet with plenty of floor space. All of the bedrooms access a well-equipped bath featuring a whirlpool tub, a relaxing shower, and a large vanity for optimal storage space.

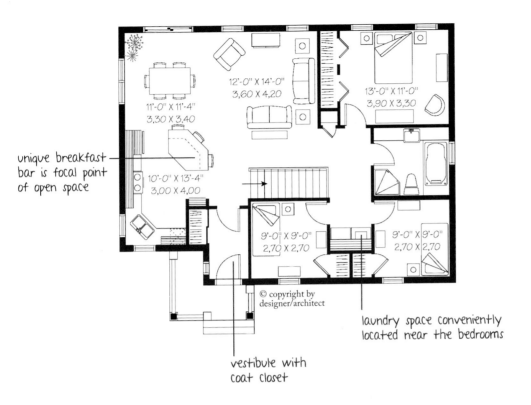

unique breakfast bar is focal point of open space

12'-0" X 14'-0"
3,60 X 4,20

11'-0" X 11'-4"
3,30 X 3,40

13'-0" X 11'-0"
3,90 X 3,30

10'-0" X 13'-4"
3,00 X 4,00

9'-0" X 9'-0"
2,70 X 2,70

9'-0" X 9'-0"
2,70 X 2,70

© copyright by designer/architect

laundry space conveniently located near the bedrooms

vestibule with coat closet

PLAN #C20-032D-0732

1160 square feet of living area
width: 40'   depth: 30'
3 bedrooms, 1 bath
2" x 6" exterior walls
basement foundation standard;
crawl space, floating slab,
or monolithic slab available for a fee

MARCO ISLE VACATION HOME

Feel as though you are truly on vacation in the Marco Isle vacation beach home. This raised coastal home design promises great views from the rear screened lanai and also from the three sets of sliding glass doors across the rear that make a seaside breeze easily accessible from any part of the interior. An island kitchen and an open great room with a centered fireplace add great function and ambiance to the main gathering space. Two bedrooms and a full bath complete the home.

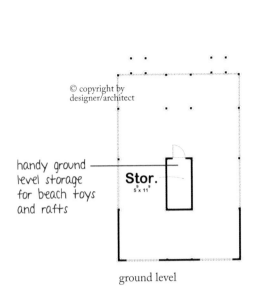

© copyright by
designer/architect

handy ground
level storage
for beach toys
and rafts

Stor.
5' x 11⁹

ground level

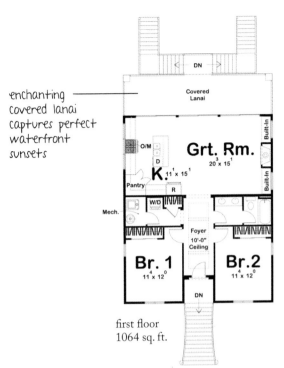

enchanting
covered lanai
captures perfect
waterfront
sunsets

DN

Covered
Lanai

O/M

D

Grt. Rm.
20³ x 15¹

Built-In

K.
11¹ x 15¹

Pantry

R

Built-In

W/D

Mech.

Foyer
10'-0"
Ceiling

Br. 1
11 x 12

Br.2
11 x 12

DN

first floor
1064 sq. ft.

PLAN #C20-123D-0128

1064 square feet of living area
width: 30'   depth: 45'
2 bedrooms, 1 bath
post and pier foundation

TEAGAN HILL VACATION HOME

The Teagan Hill vacation home has an open-concept floor plan and gathering areas with tall ceilings and towering windows above for a breezy, relaxing interior with stunning views. A second floor bedroom with loft maintain privacy. The open kitchen has a large island overlooking the great room and beyond onto the wraparound covered porch outdoors. Whether you're outside in the shade of the porch, or indoors staying cool, you will be surrounded in vacation home vibes. No, you're not dreaming, you have found your very own paradise, so start packing your bags!

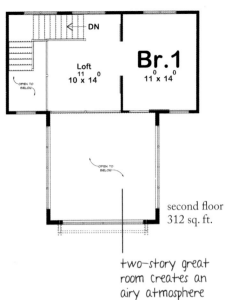

DN

Loft
11
10 x 14 0

Br.1
0   0
11 x 14 0

OPEN TO BELOW

OPEN TO BELOW

second floor
312 sq. ft.

two-story great
room creates an
airy atmosphere

Pantry

R

UP

K.
7
15 x 8
5
D

Grt. Rm.
7   4
15 x 17
2 Story Ceiling

family
favorite
wraparound
porch

© copyright by
designer/architect

Covered
Porch

first floor
687 sq. ft.

PLAN #C20-123D-0085

999 square feet of living area
width: 29'   depth: 37'
1 bedrooms, 1 bath
slab foundation standard; crawl space,
basement or walk-out basement
available for a fee

WATERVISTA VACATION HOME

Whether you spend a weekend canoeing or having s'mores out by the fire pit, this bungalow-style cabin is the perfect humble abode you've always wanted to escape to. With its welcoming covered front porch for enjoying morning coffee, you'll discover that views can be seen in all directions. The main gathering space merges dining, cooking, and relaxing together, making the home feel inviting and larger than its true size. Two bedrooms also share a central bath for extra convenience. Grab your family and friends and have a fun-filled weekend at Watervista!

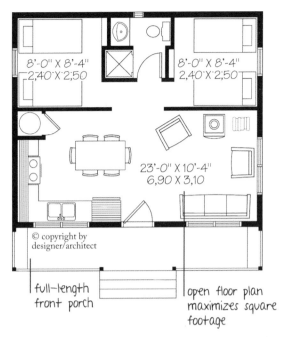

8'-0" X 8'-4"
2,40 X 2,50

8'-0" X 8'-4"
2,40 X 2,50

23'-0" X 10'-4"
6,90 X 3,10

© copyright by designer/architect

full-length front porch

open floor plan maximizes square footage

PLAN #C20-032D-0709

480 square feet of living area
width: 24'   depth: 20'
2 bedrooms, 1 bath
2" x 6" exterior walls
screw pile foundation standard;
crawl space, floating slab,
or monolithic slab available for a fee

HINES PEAK VACATION HOME

Hines Peak is a stunning, modern-style, multi-level vacation home offering privacy for the homeowner with the master bedroom located on the top floor and featuring its own walk-in closet, private bath, and sunning balcony. The first floor is one large space that is composed of dining, living, and cooking areas. Parties will be relaxing and fun thanks to the ease in which you can move through this space. The first floor leads onto a partially covered balcony that is sure to be a focal point. It will be the perfect spot for alfresco dining, sunbathing, or happy hour with guests. An optional lower level can be finished as needed and provides an additional 512 square feet of living area and offers the ability to add another living area, as well as two additional bedrooms and a bath.

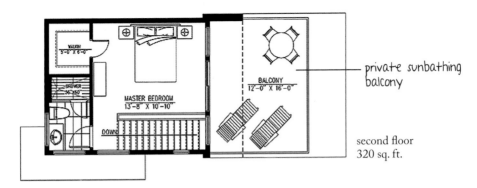

private sunbathing balcony

second floor
320 sq. ft.

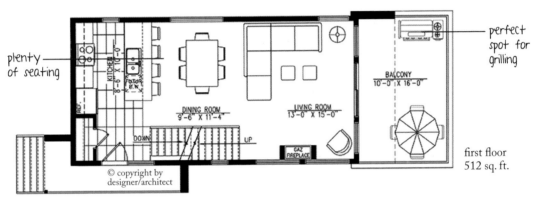

plenty of seating

perfect spot for grilling

© copyright by designer/architect

first floor
512 sq. ft.

optional lower level
512 sq. ft.

PLAN #C20-148D-0032

832 square feet of living area
512 bonus square feet
width: 16'   depth: 32'
1 bedroom, 1 bath
2" x 6" exterior walls
walk-out basement foundation

GRAY LAKE VACATION HOME

Pack up for the weekend and stay at the Gray Lake vacation spot, where you can hunt, fish, or just enjoy nature to the fullest. This vacation getaway offers luxury for its size that includes a kitchen with large island, a second floor bedroom and a luxury bath featuring an oversized easily accessible walk-in shower. There is also a wonderful covered porch, perfect for relaxing outdoors without the heat of direct sunlight. Sneak away to the Gray Lake and come back refreshed and ready for the week ahead!

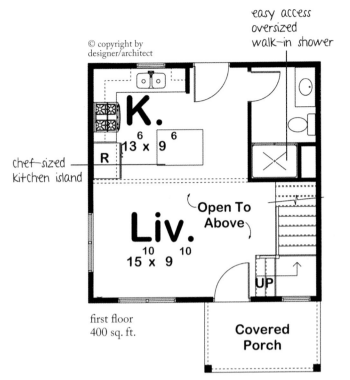

© copyright by designer/architect

easy access oversized walk-in shower

chef-sized kitchen island

K.
13 x 9

R

Liv.
15 x 9

Open To Above

UP

first floor
400 sq. ft.

Covered Porch

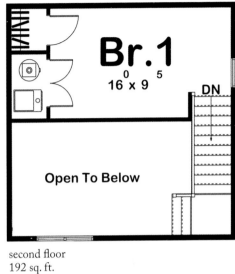

Br.1
16 x 9

DN

Open To Below

second floor
192 sq. ft.

PLAN #C20-123D-0029

592 square feet of living area
width: 20'   depth: 26'
1 bedroom, 1 bath
slab foundation standard; crawl space,
basement or walk-out basement
available for a fee

BAGNELL LAKE VACATION HOME

Head on out this weekend to the Bagnell Lake vacation home that is sure to be the envy of the cove. Designed perfectly for a sloping lot, the large vaulted living room with fireplace overlooks a huge outdoor deck. The corner kitchen is nearby so outdoor grilling and dining is easy. There's a bedroom on the first floor, and two bedrooms and a bath on the second floor. The basement can be finished to offer more bedroom or gathering space when larger crowds are invited.

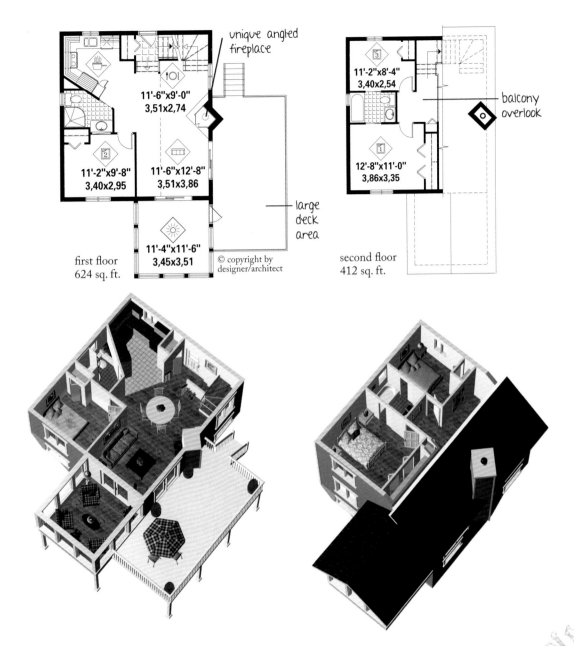

unique angled fireplace

11'-6"x9'-0"
3,51x2,74

11'-2"x9'-8"
3,40x2,95

11'-6"x12'-8"
3,51x3,86

large deck area

11'-4"x11'-6"
3,45x3,51

© copyright by designer/architect

first floor
624 sq. ft.

11'-2"x8'-4"
3,40x2,54

balcony overlook

12'-8"x11'-0"
3,86x3,35

second floor
412 sq. ft.

PLAN #C20-126D-1029

1036 square feet of living area
width: 24'   depth: 26'
3 bedrooms, 2 baths
2" x 6" exterior walls
basement foundation

ST. THOMAS VACATION HOME

Looking for your own private island oasis? The ultra-chic St. Thomas beach vacation home is the perfect beach bungalow with breezy shaded deck space in every direction. The first floor has a compact kitchen and a common living space surrounded in windows for great views. The second floor loft is accessed by a ladder and offers the perfect spot to catch some shut eye before you catch your next wave. Enjoy the tranquility and comfort of this stylish dwelling designed perfectly for beach front property. Hang ten!

wraparound covered deck

Covered Deck

K.
12 x 9

R

D

Ladder to Loft

Living
12 x 12

© copyright by designer/architect

Covered Deck

first floor
330 sq. ft.

completely private sleeping loft

W/D

Loft
12 x 12

second floor
203 sq. ft.

PLAN #C20-123D-0040

533 square feet of living area
width: 24'   depth: 39'
1 bedroom, 1 bath
crawl space foundation

RUTLEDGE LAKE VACATION HOME

The Rutledge Lake waterfront home has a stylish modern feel with rustic touches that ideally suit a waterfront locale. The floor plan ensures an open living style with the kitchen and family room combining and an oversized island providing dining and prepping space. The lower level has a handy garage style storage space that can hold rafts, canoes and other fun water accessories. Life will be far from boring at the Rutledge Lake vacation home.

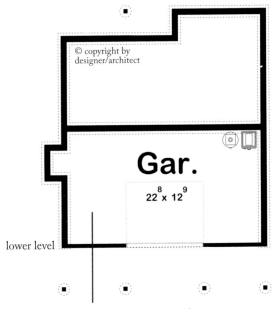

© copyright by
designer/architect

Gar.

22⁸ x 12⁹

lower level

handy garage for boat storage
or other lake necessities

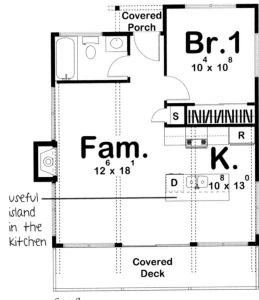

Covered
Porch

Br.1
10⁴ x 10⁸

S

R

Fam.
12⁶ x 18¹

K.
10⁸ x 13⁰

useful
island
in the
kitchen

D

Covered
Deck

first floor
624 sq. ft.

PLAN #C20-123D-0080

609 square feet of living area
width: 26'   depth: 32'
1 bedroom, 1 bath
walk-out basement standard; crawl space, slab or
basement available for a fee

WOODBRIDGE

The Woodbridge is a great starter or vacation home, with its completely open living and dining areas making it feel larger than its actual size. The convenient U-shaped kitchen has a breakfast bar. The living/dining area opens to a spacious deck where enjoying the outdoors is a breeze. Quite possibly the perfect cabin!

PLAN #C20-001D-0086

1154 square feet of living area
width: 28'   depth: 30'
3 bedrooms, 1½ baths
crawl space standard;
basement or slab available for a fee

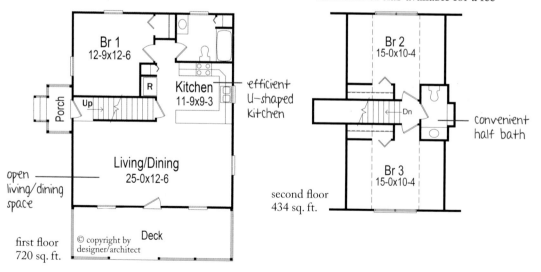

Br 1
12-9x12-6

Kitchen
11-9x9-3

Porch

Up

R

efficient U-shaped Kitchen

open living/dining space

Living/Dining
25-0x12-6

© copyright by designer/architect

Deck

first floor
720 sq. ft.

Br 2
15-0x10-4

Dn

convenient half bath

Br 3
15-0x10-4

second floor
434 sq. ft.

ALFREDO LAGO

PLAN #C20-011D-0291

972 square feet of living area
width: 49'-6"   depth: 31'-6"
1 bedroom, 1 bath
2" x 6" exterior walls
crawl space or slab standard;
basement available for a fee

Dreaming of an Italian villa high in the hills of wine country? Look no further than this Tuscan-inspired villa with the romance and character to create the feeling of complete bliss in a faraway place. A pergola-style outdoor living space has multiple sliding glass doors leading to the living room with a freestanding fireplace. A sizable kitchen with eating bar makes Italian recipes a cinch, and the bedroom is spacious with direct bath access. Feel as though you've been whisked away in stunning Tuscan style with the Alfredo Lago!

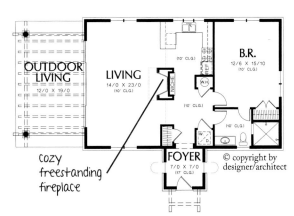

cozy freestanding fireplace

OUTDOOR LIVING
12/0 X 19/0

LIVING
14/0 X 23/0
(10' CLG.)

B.R.
12/6 X 15/10
(10' CLG.)

FOYER
7/0 X 7/0

© copyright by designer/architect

YAKUTAT

Memorable family events are certain to be enjoyed on the partially covered deck of the Yakutat vacation home. The living area is topped with a cathedral ceiling and rafters for a dramatic, open feel. A kitchenette, bedroom, and bath complete the first floor, while a second floor loft is accessible by an incline ladder. Relaxing is sure to be a breeze in this retreat-like A-frame home.

PLAN #C20-008D-0161

618 square feet of living area
width: 20'   depth: 30'
1 bedroom, 1 bath
pier foundation

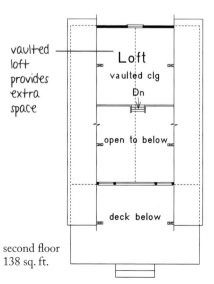

first floor
480 sq. ft.

© copyright by designer/architect

second floor
138 sq. ft.

HIDDEN COTTAGE

PLAN #C20-144D-0013

624 square feet of living area
width: 24'   depth: 36'
1 bedroom, 1 bath
2" x 6" exterior walls
slab foundation standard;
crawl space available for a fee

The Hidden Cottage Craftsman vacation home has tons of curb appeal! The living room enjoys plenty of natural light from multiple windows. The kitchen has a center island overlooking the living room that includes a snack bar for hanging out. Pocket doors separate the mud room from the bathroom and kitchen with a space saving layout.

functional mud room

easy snack bar

BLUESTONE

The Bluestone keeps vacation life as simple as can be with its effortless layout and small footprint. Triple sliding glass doors reveal a large covered porch, perfect for an early morning coffee as the sun rises. An easy to access walk-in shower makes it easy for all physical abilities to visit and enjoy this home and the bathroom is only steps from the bedroom for convenience any time of the day or night. The efficient galley-style kitchen is hassle-free making cooking at home feel less like a chore.

PLAN #C20-123D-0078

485 square feet of living area
width: 22'-4"   depth: 26'-8"
1 bedroom, 1 bath
slab foundation standard; crawl space, basement or walk-out basement available for a fee

© copyright by designer/architect

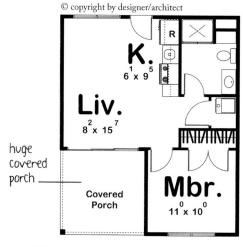

K.
6 x 9

Liv.
8 x 15

Mbr.
11 x 10

huge covered porch

Covered Porch

COBBS COVE

PLAN #C20-144D-0024

1024 square feet of living area
width: 32'   depth: 32'
1 bedroom, 1½ baths
2" x 6" exterior walls
crawl space, slab or basement foundation
standard; walk-out basement for a fee

Settle in around the fire pit and enjoy the large deck at Cobbs Cove. This smaller sized dwelling has a great layout for a mother-in-law home, vacation spot, or anyone looking to downsize. The master bedroom is spacious and has a walk-in closet, a private bath with a double vanity and a shower designed to handle a roll-in wheelchair.

handicap accessible bathroom

CLAIRE BEACH

Retreat to Claire Beach and find your happy place. The modern, sleek style will make living uncomplicated and less stressful. The vaulted living area is two stories tall with towering windows so you can enjoy views of the beach or lake shore. Two bedrooms, one on each floor, offer maximum privacy.

PLAN #C20-126D-1037

1165 square feet of living area
width: 26' depth: 28'
2 bedrooms, 2 baths
2" x 6" exterior walls
basement foundation

8'-6"x11'-4"
2,59x3,45

8'-4"x11'-8"
2,54x3,56

open family
living space

23'-0"x12'-0"
7,01x3,66

© copyright by
designer/architect

first floor
688 sq. ft.

12'-0"x11'-4"
3,66x3,45

space-
saving
pocket
doors

loft open
to below

12'-0"x15'-4"
3,66x4,67

second floor
477 sq. ft.

THOMPSON FALLS

PLAN #C20-123D-0064

1194 square feet of living area
width: 62'   depth: 51'
1 bedroom, 1 bath
slab foundation standard;
crawl space, basement or
walk-out basement
available for a fee

Escape the daily stress of life at the Thompson Falls vacation home! Designed with a nod to the popular Modern Farmhouse style, this trendy dwelling has an open, relaxed floor plan ready for all of the challenges and action of waterfront living. Enjoy views in every direction on the covered porch and take in waterfront vistas from the second floor loft with a cathedral ceiling. Plus, the two-car garage will be handy when the teenage kids arrive on the weekend.

second floor
273 sq. ft.

loft open to below

first floor
921 sq. ft.

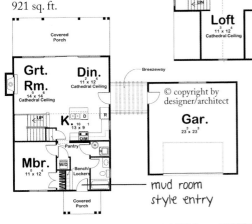

mud room style entry

BIG SKY PEAK

The Big Sky Peak is a modern masterpiece perfect for great views, whether mountain or coastal. With its huge deck and wall of windows, no view is left unseen. The first floor includes an island kitchen as well as the master bedroom and a full bath. An optional lower level doubles the square footage and includes three additional bedrooms, a large bath, and washer/dryer closet.

PLAN #C20-148D-0047

720 square feet of living area
720 bonus square feet
width: 30'   depth: 24'
1 bedroom, 1 bath
2" x 6" exterior walls
basement foundation

useful carport

wall of windows

double bowl vanity

BEDROOM #2
12'-8" X 10'-0"

BEDROOM #3
10'-0" X 12'-4"

OPTIONAL

CARPORT
12'-0" X 28'-0"

BATH

STORAGE

BEDROOM #4/FAMILY ROOM
10'-0" X 10'-0"

© copyright by designer/architect

optional lower level
720 sq. ft.

KITCHEN
8'-6" X 12'-8"

MASTER BEDROOM
10'-0" X 12'-4"

DINING ROOM
9'-10" X 10'-8"

TERRASSE
12'-0" X 28'-0"

CATHEDRAL CEILING

LIVING ROOM
13'-0" X 12'-0"

BATH

first floor
720 sq. ft.

JUNIPER COVE

PLAN #C20-126D-1022

1156 square feet of living area
width: 24'   depth: 28'
2 bedrooms, 1 bath
2" x 6" exterior walls
basement foundation

Juniper Cove offers the perfect setup for lakeside living since it's designed ideally for a sloping lot. With a layout perfect for rear views, the bedrooms all enjoy balconies or large windows for catching sunsets over the water. Window walls make guests and family feel one with nature even if they're indoors by the fire.

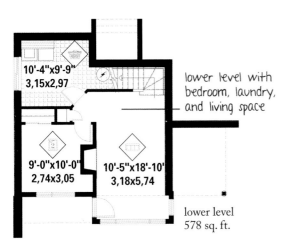

10'-4"x9'-9"
3,15x2,97

lower level with bedroom, laundry, and living space

9'-0"x10'-0"
2,74x3,05

10'-5"x18'-10"
3,18x5,74

lower level
578 sq. ft.

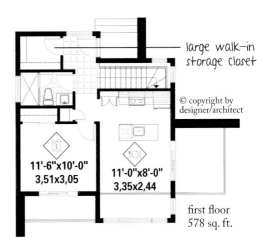

large walk-in storage closet

© copyright by
designer/architect

11'-6"x10'-0"
3,51x3,05

11'-0"x8'-0"
3,35x2,44

first floor
578 sq. ft.

SHADYBRIDGE LAKE

Shadybridge Lake is a low-maintenance cottage offering vacation living with 2" x 6" exterior walls. The living/dining area merges with the kitchen. This plan also has an uninsulated/unheated version for seasonal use only.

PLAN #C20-032D-0708

400 square feet of living area
width: 20' depth: 20'
1 bedroom, 1 bath
screw pile foundation standard;
crawl space, monolithic slab, or floating slab
available for a fee

SCENIC POINT Modern cabin-style

living has never been easier than with the Scenic Point. The front screen porch creates ideal outdoor living space, while two bedrooms share a full bath with an efficient and convenient washer/dryer space.

PLAN #C20-126D-1018

900 square feet of living area
width: 30' depth: 42'
2 bedrooms, 1 bath
2" x 6" exterior walls
basement foundation

BIXBY LANE The covered patio offers

a tranquil spot to take in the surrounding views. Inside, an expansive living room is open to the kitchen, creating an ideal entertaining spot with a center eating island.

PLAN #C20-144D-0017

1043 square feet of living area
width: 42' depth: 34'-6"
2 bedrooms, 1 bath
2" x 6" exterior walls
crawl space standard; slab for a fee

WINDFALL RIDGE This cozy,

quaint cabin has 2" x 6" exterior walls and Craftsman details, making it irresistible. One gathering area with a centered fireplace blends with the kitchen for relaxed cabin living.

PLAN #C20-032D-0710

540 square feet of living area
width: 18' depth: 30'
2 bedrooms, 1 bath
screw pile foundation standard;
crawl space, monolithic slab, or floating slab
available for a fee

HIGHLANDER
The perfect cabin for comfort and utility. Abundant windows in the gathering area provide sunlight throughout. The U-shaped kitchen has a breakfast bar opening to the living area. The large covered deck offers plenty of outdoor living space.

PLAN #C20-001D-0085
720 square feet of living area
width: 28' depth: 38'
2 bedrooms, 1 bath
crawl space foundation standard;
slab available for a fee

BASS HARBOR
This friendly Craftsman bungalow has a rear covered porch off the well-planned kitchen, offering a great location for a grill. The open dining area flows into the family room with fireplace. A walk-in closet and private bath are found in the master bedroom.

PLAN #C20-026D-1833
1195 square feet of living area
width: 40' depth: 48'-8"
3 bedrooms, 2 baths
basement foundation standard;
crawl space, slab, or walk-out basement
available for a fee

STILLBROOK
What a great getaway with all the comforts of home! A wraparound covered deck and transomed glass doors fill the interior with light. The kitchen/dining/living area has sloped ceilings.

PLAN #C20-008D-0153
792 square feet of living area
width: 24' depth: 42'
2 bedrooms, 1 bath
crawl space standard;
slab available for a fee

GULL COVE
The Gull Cove brings back memories of days gone by and places of comfort. Snuggling by the fireplace in winter, or enjoying the breeze on the porch in summer makes this a great spot year-round.

PLAN #C20-077D-0296
872 square feet of living area
width: 32'-8" depth: 36'
1 bedroom, 1½ baths
crawl space or slab foundation, please specify
when ordering; for basement version, see
plan #077D-0297 at houseplansandmore.com

WINTERS TRAIL
Double fireplaces keep the Winters Trail cabin cozy end to end whether you're in the vaulted sitting area, or in the large bunk room with enough space for multiple bunk beds, this cabin is sure to be the spot for fun sleep-overs with family and friends.

PLAN #C20-058D-0242
772 square feet of living area
width: 35'-4"   depth: 31'-8"
1 bedroom, 1 bath
crawl space foundation

PACIFIC CREST
The Pacific Crest has the perfect no-fuss layout. The open kitchen has dining space and family room views. A bedroom with bath provide a nice spot to fall asleep each night and the bunk room has space for up to eight allowing for weekend visitors.

PLAN #C20-123D-0096
1096 square feet of living area
width: 30'   depth: 38'
2 bedrooms, 1 bath
slab foundation standard; crawl space, basement or walk-out basement available for a fee

MOONLIGHT BAY
A great modern cabin with a floor plan filled with natural light and interesting angles. The kitchen has dining space and a gathering space with a corner fireplace off the other side.

PLAN #C20-126D-0988
850 square feet of living area
width: 34'   depth: 30'
2 bedrooms, 1 bath
2" x 6" exterior walls
slab foundation

PROCTOR
Striking and sleek, the interior is light and open with a two-story living room, while the exterior walls are 2" x 6" for efficiency. The kitchen has a built-in table and the second floor has two bedrooms.

PLAN #C20-032D-0863
1200 square feet of living area
width: 27'-7"   depth: 28'
2 bedrooms, 2 baths
2" x 6" exterior walls
crawl space foundation standard;
monolithic slab or floating slab available for a fee

OZARK SPRINGS
Although small in size, the Ozark Springs dwelling is big when it comes to style! Great, sun-filled one-level living including a large balcony/deck will make sunbathing a cinch. Soak up the sun in this amazing design!

PLAN #C20-141D-0315
750 square feet of living area
width: 25'   depth: 40'
1 bedroom, 1 bath
2" x 6" exterior walls
pier foundation

SUNDANCE HILL
A wrap-around covered deck surrounds this fun, rustic cabin with tons of space for sunning, grilling and relaxing. The cozy great room is where the action is and has views in every direction.

PLAN #C20-123D-0083
968 square feet of living area
width: 43'   depth: 31'
2 bedrooms, 2 baths
crawl space foundation standard

BEAVERHILL
Lots of glass and a low roofline create a retreat you'll be begging to return to. The living room has a fireplace that heats a nearby stone wall for extra warmth. The kitchen has dining space.

PLAN #C20-008D-0133
624 square feet of living area
width: 26'   depth: 24'
2 bedrooms, 1 bath
pier foundation

SHADY SLOPE
The perfect option for a sloping lot, whether mountain or lakeside, this home offers a comfortable gathering space, a sunny dining area, and a kitchen with a laundry room.

PLAN #C20-126D-1005
1133 square feet of living area
width: 42'   depth: 32'
2 bedrooms, 1 1/2 baths
2" x 6" exterior walls
basement foundation

"RIGHT-SIZING" YOUR HOME & LIFE

When you call out to another family member, does your home seem to echo? Are there more spaces that aren't used in your home than are being used? Like many homeowners who once thought "bigger is better," you may be changing your tune. Many of us are changing our ways and learning that downsizing is the way to go. And, thanks to the recession in the not-so-distant past, we have learned that it is possible to have simplicity in our lives, spend less money, and still enjoy a very full life.

Once considered standard practice for empty nesters and retirees only, downsizing is now reaching all ages and incomes and it is for a variety of reasons. Many have chosen to downsize their home because they want a simpler lifestyle with less maintenance. People who love to travel or who are involved with many hobbies outside their home want less clutter and maintenance in their everyday life. Downsizing has also come to the forefront of society because of those who have faced financial difficulties in the past several years. Many homeowners have had no choice but to downsize and rid themselves of expensive mortgages in order to make ends meet. Whatever the situation, there are several advantages to downsizing that may convince you that it is the right choice for you and your family.

ADVANTAGES OF DOWNSIZING

Increased Cash Flow
Whether you shrink your mortgage or you use the proceeds of selling your current home to pay entirely for a new smaller home, you will end up with more money in your pocket for saving, investing, or spending in another way. Cutting your housing costs is an instant way to increase your savings. So, whether you retire in five years or you're just starting out, think about the added security a smaller home will bring to your financial future.

More Time
Less rooms and smaller ones will cut the time it takes to keep your home maintained more than you might think. Use all this free time for something you really enjoy.

Lower Utility Bills

Yes, this goes along with increased cash flow, but typically smaller homes don't have as much wasted space, so you will be living more efficiently. Using less energy while keeping your home comfortable means lower utility bills.

Reduced Consumption of Everything

From electric and gas to furniture and home accessories, if there is no place to put it, you will think twice before buying it. That means you will automatically spend less on food, clothing, and consumer goods, probably without really noticing.

Less Stress

A smaller home means less responsibility with chores, hefty maintenance bills, and other monthly obligations as a homeowner. Those who successfully downsize appear happier when they are no longer overwhelmed by the high demand and expense of a larger home.

YOU'VE MADE YOUR DECISION, NOW WHAT?

Before you put up a For Sale sign on your current home's front lawn, it is wise to understand how you spend your money, so even when you downsize you still don't find yourself financially strapped. Perhaps you and your family spend way too much money going out to dinner. Well, a smaller home will help, but if freeing up some money for your savings or other reasons is your goal, you may have to examine your lifestyle and see if any changes in how you live are in order. This may be the perfect time to decide what you want to spend your money on and then cut out the things that aren't really important to you.

Remember, downsizing and moving isn't easy. It represents a significant change that no doubt will be physically and emotionally draining during the process, but when "right-sizing" into a smaller home, it will be well worth it in the end. Downsizing is meant to simplify your life, not complicate it. So look forward to a clean, clutter-free home that requires less maintenance and less money to maintain making your family's life happier and easier overall.

SMALL
HOMES

Plan #C20-032D-0904 is found on page 132.

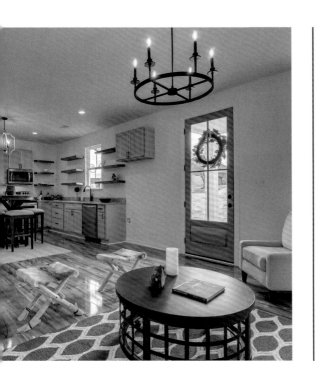

Offering everything a homeowner wants in a smaller footprint with less maintenance, small homes are a very popular trend right now. From new modern designs, to timeless traditional styles, homeowners have discovered that less is more and are choosing this as a way of life. If a small home offers the efficiency and function every homeowner needs, then why do you need more? These small homes look great built anywhere, city or country, and they have all the comfort and amenities you've come to expect from our carefully curated collection of home designs.

FARGO FALLS SMALL HOME

This rustic beauty provides plenty of space in a small amount of square footage. Step into the living/dining space and notice the large amount of windows on one wall adding a tremendous amount of sunlight. A small yet efficient kitchen offers all of the essentials for cooking daily meals. One bedroom is found on the first floor near a full bath, and two other bedrooms and a full bath reside on the second floor for extra privacy. Two additional spaces for storage make the Fargo Falls small home easy to downsize to.

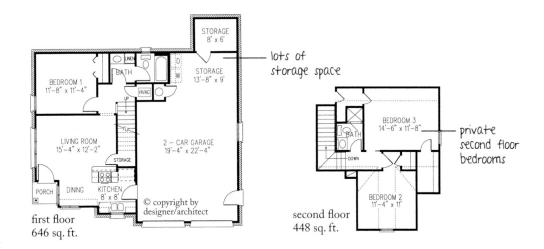

BEDROOM 1
11'-8" x 11'-4"

BATH

LIN

D
W

STORAGE
8' x 6'

STORAGE
13'-8" x 9'

HVAC

UP

lots of
storage space

LIVING ROOM
15'-4" x 12'-2"

STORAGE

2 – CAR GARAGE
19'-4" x 22'-4"

PORCH

DINING

KITCHEN
8' x 8'

© copyright by
designer/architect

first floor
646 sq. ft.

BEDROOM 3
14'-6" x 11'-8"

BATH

DOWN

private
second floor
bedrooms

BEDROOM 2
11'-4" x 11'

second floor
448 sq. ft.

PLAN #C20-137D-0271

1094 square feet of living area
width: 41'   depth: 40'
3 bedrooms, 2 baths
slab foundation

DORAL
SMALL HOME

Stylish and charming, the Doral Craftsman Modern Farmhouse inspired home has an inviting entry with space for outdoor relaxation under a covered porch. Enter the home and discover an open living room with the kitchen located behind it. The kitchen features a large breakfast bar with space for up to four people. To the left of the entry is an office/guest room with direct access to a full bath and beyond into the roomy mud room. To the right of the entry is the master bedroom with a handicap accessible bath and a walk-in closet. Quite possibly the perfect in-law, or granny pod!

large mud room

versatile office/guest room

© copyright by designer/architect

DOUBLE GARAGE 20-0 x 23-0

MUD ROOM 11-1 x 6-10

KITCHEN 13-0 x 10-6

WALK IN CLOSET 11-8 x 4-6

BATH

OFFICE / GUEST 11-1 x 10-6

MASTER BEDROOM 11-8 x 11-3

LIVING ROOM 13-0 x 14-6

PLAN #C20-144D-0023

928 square feet of living area
width: 58'   depth: 32'
2 bedrooms, 2 baths
2" x 6" exterior walls
crawl space or slab standard; basement or walk-out
basement available for a fee

LILY LAKE SMALL HOME

The Lily Lake has so much style and function you won't miss the square footage. Enter from the covered wraparound porch and find a kitchen with great room views. The two-story great room with a cozy fireplace opens onto the spacious covered porch, perfect for summertime entertaining or dining alfresco. A second floor loft is the ideal home office space away from the first floor activity and noise. Small home living has never seemed so appealing until now!

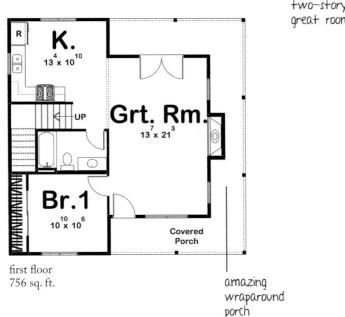

K.
13⁴ x 10¹⁰

R

UP

Grt. Rm.
13⁷ x 21³

Br.1
10¹⁰ x 10⁶

Covered Porch

first floor
756 sq. ft.

amazing wraparound porch

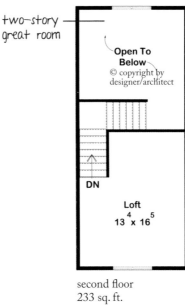

two-story great room

Open To Below
© copyright by designer/architect

DN

Loft
13⁴ x 16⁵

second floor
233 sq. ft.

PLAN #C20-123D-0086

989 square feet of living area
width: 33'   depth: 31'-8"
1 bedroom, 1 bath
crawl space foundation

CAMILLE HILL
SMALL HOME

The Camille Hill small home takes simplicity and style to a new level. Step into the entry from the covered front porch and discover an oversized walk-in closet for keeping the entry clutter-free. The open-concept floor plan has the kitchen and dining area blended perfectly. The kitchen has a large walk-in pantry with a barn style door for a inviting farmhouse feel. The bedroom enjoys close proximity to the pampering bath featuring a shower as well as a free-standing tub in one corner. This home may be small, but it's full of luxury!

© copyright by designer/architect

11'-0" x 12'-0"

11'-0" x 16'-0"

10'-8" x 12'-0"

walk-in pantry

first floor
1178 sq. ft.

13'-10" x 12'-0"

13'-2" x 8'-2"

PLAN #C20-032D-0963

1178 square feet of living area
1178 bonus square feet
width: 34'   depth: 38'
1 bedroom, 1 bath
2" x 6" exterior walls
basement foundation standard;
crawl space, floating slab
or monolithic slab available for a fee

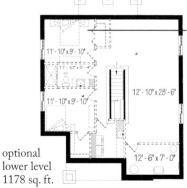

11'-10" x 9'-10"

11'-10" x 5'-4"

11'-10" x 9'-10"

12'-10" x 28'-6"

great flexible space

12'-6" x 7'-0"

optional
lower level
1178 sq. ft.

EMMIT CREEK
SMALL HOME

Emmit Creek is an ideal layout for a vacation home, or a home for a small family. Its welcoming open interior spaces will feel larger than their true size and create a natural feeling of spaciousness. The kitchen island will offer that much needed prep and extra dining space, maximizing function. Two bedrooms share the full bath tucked between them. This simple yet fluid open-concept floor plan reminds all of us that less is certainly more.

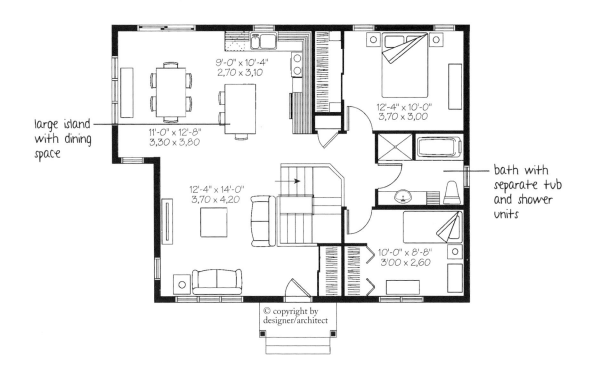

9'-0" x 10'-4"
2,70 x 3,10

12'-4" x 10'-0"
3,70 x 3,00

large island
with dining
space

11'-0" x 12'-8"
3,30 x 3,80

bath with
separate tub
and shower
units

12'-4" x 14'-0"
3,70 x 4,20

10'-0" x 8'-8"
3'00 x 2,60

© copyright by
designer/architect

PLAN #C20-032D-0904

975 square feet of living area
width: 37'   depth: 28'
2 bedrooms, 1 bath
2" x 6" exterior walls
basement foundation standard;
crawl space, floating slab,
or monolithic slab available for a fee

KILLARNEY BAY SMALL HOME

If you're looking for endless country-style charm, then Killarney Bay is just the home for you. A sizable vaulted living area welcomes you inside and flows into the rear kitchen with a spacious area for dining. The luxurious bath includes both a walk-in shower and a garden tub, making this gem of a home a rare find for comfort and unexpected elegance. Two generously sized bedrooms provide plenty of personal space for all of your belongings. There are no sacrifices when living in this small treasure.

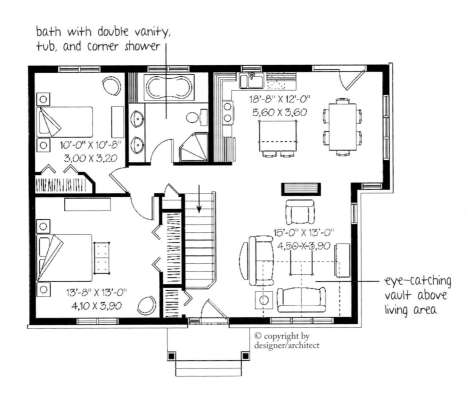

bath with double vanity, tub, and corner shower

10'-0" X 10'-8"
3,00 X 3,20

18'-8" X 12'-0"
5,60 X 3,60

15'-0" X 13'-0"
4,50 X 3,90

13'-8" X 13'-0"
4,10 X 3,90

eye-catching vault above living area

© copyright by designer/architect

PLAN #C20-032D-0945

1068 square feet of living area
width: 40'   depth: 28'
2 bedrooms, 1 bath
2" x 6" exterior walls
basement foundation standard;
crawl space, floating slab,
or monolithic slab available for a fee

DEBRAY SMALL HOME

The Debray is a compact ranch home with an open floor plan that merges dining, living, and cooking into one main gathering space. Two bedrooms share a centrally located full bath with ease, and the bath features a laundry room wall. A coat closet is found by the front entry and a walk-in pantry is located in the kitchen behind a barn style door to maximize space. Sliding glass doors off the dining area add light and outdoor access to a patio. Straightforward and functional, this small home promises to make life easy and comfortable. And, if the need arises, there's plenty of space to expand in the lower level.

luxury bath with built-in laundry room wall

PATIO
8'-0" X 5'-0"

DINING ROOM
9'-8" X 13'-8"

LIVING ROOM
12'-3" X 13'-8"

KITCHEN
8'-0" X 9'-6"

PANTRY
7'-4" X 2'-10"

BEDROOM #1
12'-0" X 11'-4"

BEDROOM #2
9'-2" X 10'-8"

HALL
4'-8" X 7'-0"

STOOP
7'-4" X 5'-8"

first floor
998 sq. ft.

© copyright by designer/architect

optional
lower level
998 sq. ft.

versatile lower level adds room to grow

PLAN #C20-032D-1150

998 square feet of living area
998 bonus square feet
width: 41'-8" depth: 28'
2 bedrooms, 1 bath
2" x 6" exterior walls
basement foundation standard;
crawl space, floating slab,
or monolithic slab available for a fee

GETTY HILL SMALL HOME

The Getty Hill is filled with amenities homeowners love. An attractive Modern Farmhouse style exterior greets guests and offers simple, understated curb appeal. The living room, dining room and kitchen combination create the open-concept layout that is so desirable. The first floor also comes complete with a stylish centrally located bath. Two bedrooms provide the perfect quiet place to relax and unwind with a well-appointed master bedroom featuring a walk-in closet in one corner. This home can even expand with space in the lower level if you need to double your square footage.

walk-in kitchen pantry

DECK

BEDROOM 2
12-0 X 9-2

PANTRY

KITCHEN
10-0 X 12-0

DINING ROOM
9-0 X 12-0

BATHROOM

LIVING ROOM
15-2 X 13-0

MASTER BED.
12-4 X 13-0

WALK-IN

PORCH
8-0 X 4-0

first floor
1050 sq. ft.

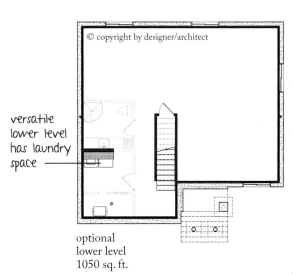

© copyright by designer/architect

versatile lower level has laundry space

optional lower level
1050 sq. ft.

PLAN #C20-032D-1107

1050 square feet of living area
1050 bonus square feet
width: 35' depth: 33'
2 bedrooms, 1 bath
2" x 6" exterior walls
basement foundation standard;
crawl space, floating slab,
or monolithic slab available for a fee

The Eureka berm home is a fresh, modern design that enjoys sleek window lines and a stucco exterior, making it truly efficient and low-maintenance. The compact U-shaped kitchen offers a tremendous amount of counterspace within reach for all sort of kitchen tasks at hand. A tall sloped ceiling in the two-story living room gives this home an open and spacious feel that all those who enter will definitely appreciate. A designated laundry room with pocket doors to a full bath is a highly functional prized feature.

convenient
main floor
bedroom

Bedroom 2
11-9x11-4

Dining
9-4x7-8

Kitchen
9-0x9-0

P

R

DW

Hall

L

Bath

Up

W

D

Lndry

Living Rm
17-8x14-11

Sloped Clg.

Foyer

© copyright by
designer/architect

Patio

first floor
880 sq. ft.

Private
bedroom with
half bath

Bath

Bedroom 1
11-10x14-2

Dn

L

Open

second floor
225 sq. ft.

PLAN #C20-122D-0001

1105 square feet of living area
width: 33'   depth: 35'
2 bedrooms, 1$\frac{1}{2}$ baths
slab foundation

BRIARWOOD
SMALL HOME

The Briarwood is famous for its open and spacious living and dining areas for family gatherings, plus a well-organized kitchen with an abundance of cabinetry and a built-in pantry for ease with storage and when entertaining. There is also a spacious deck, perfect for a grill or outdoor dining. The roomy master bath features a double-bowl vanity. A rear entry drive under garage provides space for two vehicles.

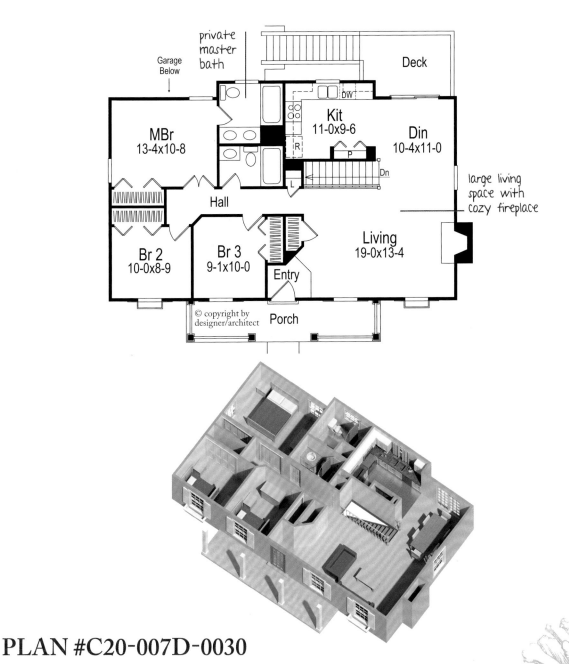

private master bath

Garage Below

Deck

MBr
13-4x10-8

Kit
11-0x9-6

Din
10-4x11-0

dw

R

P

L

Dn

large living space with cozy fireplace

Hall

Br 2
10-0x8-9

Br 3
9-1x10-0

Living
19-0x13-4

Entry

© copyright by designer/architect

Porch

PLAN #C20-007D-0030

1140 square feet of living area
width: 46'   depth: 32'
3 bedrooms, 2 baths
basement foundation standard;
crawl space or slab available for a fee

PARSON FIELD

Looking for your very own Craftsman cottage? Then Parson Field is it! Craftsman details and a covered front porch provide the utmost style and charm. The open living/dining area enjoys a cozy fireplace and a nearby U-shaped kitchen with a laundry closet near the garage. Upstairs, there are two vaulted bedrooms, a built-in desk, and a well-designed shared bath.

PLAN #C20-011D-0612

803 square feet of living area
width: 29'   depth: 29'
2 bedrooms, 1½ baths
2" x 6" exterior walls
crawl space or slab foundation standard;
basement available for a fee

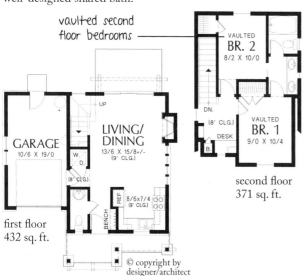

vaulted second floor bedrooms

VAULTED
BR. 2
8/2 X 10/0

DN.
(8' CLG.)

VAULTED
BR. 1
9/0 X 10/4

DESK

second floor
371 sq. ft.

UP

GARAGE
10/6 X 19/0

LIVING/
DINING
13/6 X 15/8+/-
(9' CLG.)

W.
D.
(8' CLG.)

REF

8/6x7/4
(9' CLG.)

BENCH

first floor
432 sq. ft.

© copyright by
designer/architect

LAUREL LANE

PLAN #C20-011D-0676

1196 square feet of living area
width: 40'   depth: 55'-6"
3 bedrooms, 2 baths
2" x 6" exterior walls
crawl space or slab foundation standard;
basement available for a fee

The Laurel Lane small Modern Farmhouse is completely on-point when it comes to today's sought-after style and curb appeal. Packed with plenty of bedrooms as well as open gathering space, this small home can tackle the challenges of family life from day to day. The larger than expected kitchen faces into the dining area and vaulted great room and enjoys a large island, great when prepping meals, or helping the kids with homework. The solid floor plan with an amazing exterior is bound to be an all-time favorite!

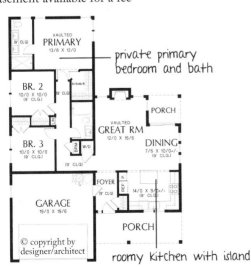

private primary bedroom and bath

roomy kitchen with island

DUNCAN FARM

Duncan Farm has a naturally welcoming feel with its covered front porch. A U-shaped kitchen and adjoining dining room seamlessly transition into the great room making the space feel larger. Double doors open to a rear patio offering space to dine or relax. The master bedroom has a walk-in closet with a private bath and easy entry to the laundry room. Two spare bedrooms have oversized closets for added storage.

PLAN #C20-077D-0208

1200 square feet of living area
width: 50'   depth: 43'
3 bedrooms, 2 baths
crawl space or slab foundation,
please specify when ordering; for
basement version, see plan #077D-0246 at
houseplansandmore.com

split
bedroom
floor plan
for privacy

large, welcoming
great room

PINECONE

PLAN #C20-008D-0148

784 square feet of living area
width: 28'   depth: 28'
3 bedrooms, 1 bath
pier foundation

Take advantage of the Pinecone's panoramic views from several different angles with this A-frame's huge wraparound deck. Upon entering the spacious living area, a cozy freestanding fireplace, a sloped ceiling, and several corner windows catch the eye. Also, the charming kitchen features a peninsula counter. Three bedrooms have direct access to the living room. This is a fun, retro design with all of the appeal of Mid-Century Modern style that's becoming so popular again.

all bedrooms have a closet for easy organization

exquisite deck for entertaining outdoors

warming fireplace graces the open living room

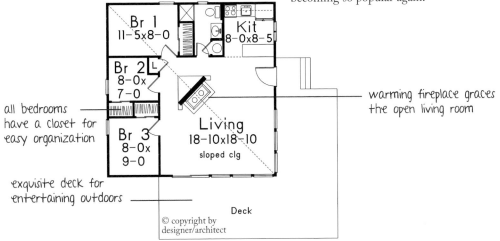

ROSEWATER

The Rosewater small home has terrific expansion possibilities in the lower level with two additional bedrooms, a full bath, and a large family room with fireplace and wet bar with island. The first floor features an open split bedroom layout ensuring privacy for all who dwell there. A mud room and separate laundry room are also great extras!

PLAN #C20-123D-0172

1192 square feet of living area
928 bonus square feet
width: 39'   depth: 48'-8"
2 bedrooms, 2 baths
basement foundation standard; crawl space, slab or walk-out basement available for a fee

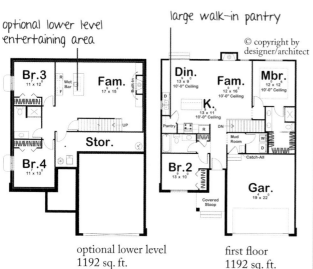

optional lower level entertaining area

large walk-in pantry

© copyright by designer/architect

optional lower level
1192 sq. ft.

first floor
1192 sq. ft.

LAURELWOOD PLACE

PLAN #C20-077D-0106

1200 square feet of living area
width: 30'   depth: 32'
3 bedrooms, 2 baths
crawl space or slab foundation,
please specify when ordering

Laurelwood Place is a great home design with very efficient use of space. This home features covered front and rear porches for enjoying those evening sunsets with family, a screened porch for comfortable dining and entertaining outdoors, a large great room, three bedrooms with walk-in closets, and even a space for the home office that you've always wanted.

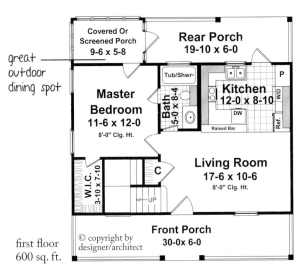

great outdoor dining spot

first floor
600 sq. ft.

© copyright by designer/architect

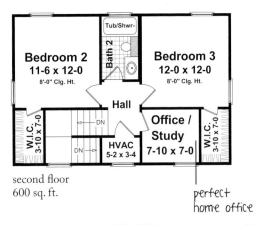

second floor
600 sq. ft.

perfect home office

TRAILBRIDGE

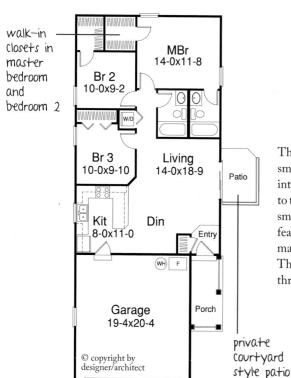

walk-in closets in master bedroom and bedroom 2

MBr
14-0x11-8

Br 2
10-0x9-2

W/D

Br 3
10-0x9-10

Living
14-0x18-9

Patio

Kit
8-0x11-0

Din

Entry

WH F

Garage
19-4x20-4

Porch

© copyright by designer/architect

private courtyard style patio

PLAN #C20-007D-0108

983 square feet of living area
width: 25'   depth: 60'
3 bedrooms, 2 baths
crawl space foundation standard;
slab available for a fee

This is an ideal home design for a narrow lot! The Trailbridge small home has a welcoming covered front porch leading you into the adorable living area and relaxing dining area that opens to the well designed kitchen with a convenient breakfast bar. A small side patio with a privacy fence creates an awesome exterior feature and is accessed from the living room. A comfortable master bedroom includes a walk-in closet and a private bath. There's even a handy washer and dryer closet right near all three bedrooms for convenience.

LAKE SIDE

PLAN #C20-130D-0411

949 square feet of living area
width: 24'   depth: 32'
1 bedroom, 1 bath
slab foundation standard;
basement or crawl space available for a fee

It's charm overload in the two-story Lake Side. Perfect as a vacation cottage or getaway spot, the Lake Side enjoys vaulted living and dining rooms, which make this home appear larger on the inside than its true size. A kitchen with an island overlooks the main gathering space. The second floor features a quiet loft, great as an artist's retreat or a home office.

© copyright by
designer/architect

two-story
living and
dining rooms

first floor
768 sq. ft.

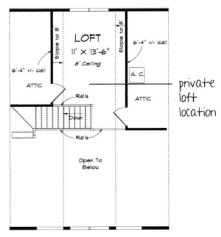

private
loft
location

second floor
181 sq. ft.

LOTUS

The Lotus small home is a wonderfully modern one-story home featuring today's open-concept floor plan everyone loves. The kitchen, living, and dining areas merge to form the core of this home. A large kitchen island ties the spaces together and creates added function and space when meal prepping. The bathroom includes washer and dryer space as well as a walk-in shower and a garden tub.

PLAN #C20-032D-0905

1146 square feet of living area
width: 40'   depth: 30'
2 bedrooms, 1 bath
2" x 6" exterior walls
basement foundation standard;
crawl space, floating slab, or monolithic slab available for a fee

huge
kitchen island

9'-4" x 11'-0"
2,80 x 3,30

10'-0" x 11'-0"
3,00 x 3,30

10'-0" x 14'-0"
3,00 x 4,20

13'-0" x 13'-0"
3,90 x 3,90

12'-0" x 14'-4"
3,60 x 4,30

© copyright by
designer/architect

MILL RIVER

Mill River stone cottage is a comfortable abode. The centered fireplace in the family room offers warmth as well as a stunning focal point. Extra dining is available at the kitchen counter near a comfortable breakfast area. Two covered porches front and back complete this special home you'll always be ready to return to.

PLAN #C20-058D-0195

923 square feet of living area
width: 36'   depth: 40'
1 bedroom, 1 bath
crawl space foundation

Bedrm
13-4x11-9

Covered Porch
7-0x10-8

Sitting
15-7x16-8

cozy fireplace is the focal point

W F
L W/D
P R Shlf
9-0x10-8
Kit

Brk fst
9-4x13-8

Covered Porch
7-0x10-8

large breakfast room near the kitchen

© copyright by designer/architect

CLEMENS COVE

The Clemens Cove small home is ideal for a sloping lot. Enter the foyer and round the corner to the great room and dining area, both comparable in size and blending together to form one large area. The kitchen has an eating bar for two and is steps from the laundry room with a built-in bench. The optional lower level and second floor allow the home to expand for future growth and includes two extra bedrooms, a family room, toy room and extra storage.

PLAN #C20-159D-0017

1200 square feet of living area
1284 bonus square feet
width: 44'   depth: 48'
2 bedrooms, 2 baths
2" x 6" exterior walls
walk-out basement foundation

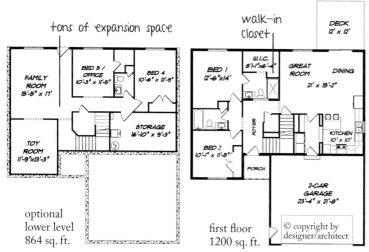

tons of expansion space

FAMILY ROOM 15'-5" x 17'

BED 5 / OFFICE 10'-3" x 11'-5"

BED 4 10'-6" x 12'-8"

TOY ROOM 11'-9" x 13'-3"

STORAGE 16'-10" x 9'-3"

optional lower level 864 sq. ft.

walk-in closet

DECK 12' x 12'

BED 1 12'-6" x 14'

W.I.C. 8'-11"x6'-4"

GREAT ROOM 21' x 15'-2"

DINING

FOYER

KITCHEN 10' x 10'

BED 2 10'-1" x 11'-5"

PORCH

2-CAR GARAGE 23'-4" x 21'-8"

© copyright by designer/architect

first floor 1200 sq. ft.

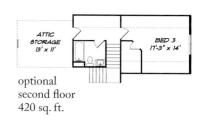

ATTIC STORAGE 13' x 11'

BED 3 17'-3" x 14'

optional second floor 420 sq. ft.

HAVERHILL LANE

PLAN #C20-011D-0446

1076 square feet of living area
width: 25'-6"   depth: 41'-6"
2 bedrooms, 2¹/₂ baths
2" x 6" exterior walls
crawl space or slab foundation standard;
basement available for a fee

Haverhill Lane will take you back in time to when homes had so much character! The welcoming wraparound covered porch leads to the dining/living area with a corner fireplace. The U-shaped kitchen has a powder room and laundry closet. Upstairs you'll discover two bedrooms, each with their own bath.

first floor
572 sq. ft.

second floor
504 sq. ft.

REF.

13/7 X 9/3
(9' CLG.)

D/W

© copyright by
designer/architect

VAULTED
BR. 2
10/7 X 10/3

LINEN

LINEN   STOR.

DINING /
LIVING
13/7 X 19/5
(9' CLG.)

VAULTED
BR. 1
13/7 X 10/9

COVERED PORCH

tons of usable
outdoor space

SAYER CREEK
Sayer Creek is bound to be your favorite getaway spot. The open layout makes the interior feel larger than expected. The kitchen even has a walk-in pantry! Two bedrooms share a bath and the back covered porch is a nice place to relax after dinner.

PLAN #C20-032D-1129
1102 square feet of living area
width: 35' depth: 34'
2 bedrooms, 1 bath
basement foundation standard;
crawl space, floating slab
or monolithic slab available for a fee

FOXPORT
A brick facade and a feature window add elegance to this narrow lot home. The vaulted living room enjoys a fireplace and opens to a U-shaped kitchen with a bayed breakfast area, snack bar, and built-in pantry.

PLAN #C20-007D-0107
1161 square feet of living area
width: 30' depth: 44'-4"
3 bedrooms, 2 baths
basement foundation

SYCAMORE BEND
Sycamore Bend makes one bedroom living feel luxurious with its vaulted, open interior, covered outdoor areas, walk-in pantry and island in the kitchen, and a bedroom with a walk-in closet.

PLAN #C20-101D-0161
744 square feet of living area
width: 35'-6" depth: 45'
1 bedroom, 1 bath
2" x 6" exterior walls
slab foundation

DEER LAKE
Deer Lake has plenty of space and a family room featuring a fireplace for added warmth. The kitchen/breakfast area feels open and bright. The bedrooms have sizable closets for great organization.

PLAN #C20-058D-0200
1185 square feet of living area
width: 36'-4" depth: 40'-4"
2 bedrooms, 2 baths
basement foundation

WINDINGPATH
This home's front and rear covered porches provide great spaces to relax with friends and family, while also extending the living space to the outdoors.

PLAN #C20-077D-0105
1100 square feet of living area
width: 31'-2" depth: 48'-6"
2 bedrooms, 2 baths
ICF exterior walls
slab foundation

DANIELS
Handsome curb appeal has been created thanks to a triple-gabled facade in the Daniels. An efficient open layout with island kitchen serves the dining and family rooms perfectly.

PLAN #C20-123D-0060
1185 square feet of living area
width: 52' depth: 38'
3 bedrooms, 2 baths
basement foundation standard; crawl space, slab or walk-out basement available for a fee

SONA
A sleek, unique getaway home ideal for a lot with a front view! The kitchen, living area, and screened porch all enjoy front views and benefit being lakefront. Two bedrooms are tucked in back for privacy and comfort.

PLAN #C20-126D-1150
600 square feet of living area
width: 30' depth: 20'
2 bedrooms, 1 bath
2" x 6" exterior walls
pilings foundation

SHERWOOD COVE
A cute, affordable home that doesn't lack curb appeal! A great starter or retirement home with open living/dining areas and a deck. The master bedroom has a walk-in closet.

PLAN #C20-051D-0889
967 square feet of living area
width: 40' depth: 44'
2 bedrooms, 1 bath
2" x 6" exterior walls
basement foundation standard;
crawl space or slab available for a fee

INDIO

There's no blending in when it comes to the Indio small home. Designed in the popular Modern Farmhouse style, this narrow lot home has three private second floor bedrooms and the first floor is drenched in sunlight from tons of windows.

PLAN #C20-111D-0042

1074 square feet of living area
width: 29'   depth: 30'
3 bedrooms, 2¹/₂ baths
slab foundation standard;
crawl space available for a fee

ROWAN PLACE

Modern style creates a special home with tons of sunlight, sloped ceilings and a refreshing personality. An open great room easily accesses the kitchen. The master bedroom has a private bath, while two additional bedrooms share a bath.

PLAN #C20-155D-0284

1074 square feet of living area
width: 35'-4"   depth: 33'-4"
3 bedrooms, 2 baths
crawl space or slab foundation, please specify when ordering

WHISTLER CIRCLE

A rustic modern masterpiece sure to brighten any neighborhood! An open floor plan with one central area for dining, cooking, and gathering. Two bedrooms share the bath.

PLAN #C20-148D-0026

938 square feet of living area
width: 32'   depth: 33'
2 bedrooms, 1 bath
2" x 6" exterior walls
basement foundation

WILLOW GATE

The Willow Gate has everything you need to enjoy life. Step into the eat-in kitchen and living room and enjoy its openness. The large walk-in closet in the bedroom will be appreciated.

PLAN #C20-101D-0164

745 square feet of living area
width: 36'-6"   depth: 34'
1 bedroom, 1 bath
2" x 6" exterior walls
crawl space foundation

GREENBAY
The entry, with convenient stairs to the basement, leads to spacious living and dining rooms open to the kitchen. The master bedroom enjoys double entry doors, a walk-in closet, and a private bath with linen closet.

PLAN #C20-007D-0181
1140 square feet of living area
width: 38'   depth: 52'-8"
3 bedrooms, 2 baths
basement foundation standard;
crawl space or slab available for a fee

FAIRLYNN
Stylish country living has never looked so good! Vaulted kitchen, living and dining rooms create an inviting open interior. Three bedrooms and two baths complete this timeless design.

PLAN #C20-141D-0476
1200 square feet of living area
width: 73'-6"   depth: 30'
3 bedrooms, 2 baths
2" x 6" exterior walls
slab foundation

MILL HOLLOW
Find your inner peace at the Mill Hollow cottage. The cozy sitting area with fireplace is a great place to start your day with a piping hot cup of coffee, or enjoy one of two covered outdoor spaces.

PLAN #C20-058D-0213
644 square feet of living area
width: 22'-8"   depth: 39'-4"
1 bedroom, 1 bath
crawl space foundation

AVALON LANE
Looking to turn heads and live in a stunning Modern home? The Avalon Lane delivers serious style while satisfying your need for a functional floor plan. What more could you ask for?

PLAN #C20-155D-0171
1131 square feet of living area
width: 53'-8"   depth: 41'-4"
3 bedrooms, 2 baths
crawl space or slab foundation,
please specify when ordering

APARTMENT GARAGE DECOR IDEAS

Apartment garage living is a great solution to many family changes. Whether you have a child home from college or you have a live-in parent who requires some assistance but can do many tasks unsupervised, a garage apartment may be the perfect fit for your family's needs. But how do you make an apartment garage feel comfortable, cozy, and functional? The last thing you want it to feel like is, well…a garage.

To make apartment garage living feel like a home, special challenges need to be met. First, square footage has to be maximized to its fullest. Apartment garages are small, so every inch of the floor plan has to be accounted for when selecting and placing furniture. An oversized sofa or L-shaped sofa may be what you want, but once you get them in a small space, they may appear too monstrous. Carefully choose furniture pieces so they are multi-functional yet comfortable. Versatile furniture pieces include futons or sofa beds that offer additional sleeping space as well as seating when entertaining. Or, use an ottoman to double as a stool for seating and add a tray on top for easy additional table space that can be placed anywhere at anytime. Stacking tables also add function by using very little floor space, but they can be separated to provide extra tables near seating areas when entertaining. Multi-functional furniture pieces will give you the extra function without overcrowding the interior with too much furniture.

Another universal challenge with garage apartments is their lack of storage. Apartment garages aren't known for having spacious walk-in closets. In fact, the closets are often tiny. So get creative with adding storage. Purchase adjustable rods and add to the closets for extra rows of hanging space. Also, install pullout rods that can be extended in the bathroom for a handy place to hang a robe or towel.

If you have a hard time finding places for items like seasonal decorations or family mementos; use the space under the bed or sofa. Raise your bed with cement blocks and add a longer bed skirt to hide them. The extra height creates more storage space while creating an elegance to your bedroom or sleeping area.

Another stylish way to add storage is to find shelves that act as decoration but also offer functionality. Shelves provide a great spot for collectibles and keep the floor space open. Whether it's a shelf with towels in the bathroom, or a shelf with books above the bed, it's functional but provides architectural interest. Browse local flea markets or yard and estate sales for one-of-a-kind shelves that create a stylish focal point.

ACCESSORIES TO OPEN UP THE SPACE

Many apartment garages have open floor plans with all of the living spaces combined. In many ways, this is a plus because additional walls separating everything would only make the interior feel even smaller. But, with all spaces as one, sometimes separation visually needs to occur to make it function properly.

Try building or buying a screen to create privacy from the sleeping area to the living space. Or remove the screen to open up the space.

Also, use rugs to visually separate the interior. Try a bold pattern such as a stripe to act as a partition between the living space and the bedroom.

Mirrors give the illusion of a larger space, no matter its size. Placing mirrors across from windows also adds extra light, meaning less need for extra lamps.

Whatever your needs may be, an apartment garage is a great solution by creating additional living space that is private yet convenient to the main home. Use these inexpensive decorating tips for small spaces and make your garage apartment feel comfortable, cozy, and functional all at the same time.

APARTMENT GARAGES
Including Garages with Lofts or Storage

Plan #C20-173D-7500 is found on page 166.

Apartment garages have taken on a whole new meaning for many families looking for flexibility today. Instead of packing up and moving when your home begins to shrink, why not stay put and build an apartment garage for the children home from college, house guests, or even the in-law no longer able to live entirely on their own? An apartment garage is the perfect solution! There are so many floor plan options, features, and architectural styles, you will have no problem finding an apartment garage that complements the architectural style of your existing home. Or, why not build an apartment garage as a vacation rental or a retirement getaway for yourself? The options are truly limitless!

CARLEY CANYON APARTMENT GARAGE

This stylish apartment garage sets itself apart from all of the others with its sleek exterior, no-nonsense style, and its open and bright, welcoming interior. The U-shaped kitchen is steps away from the open living area, with windows on every wall filling the space with an abundance of natural sunlight. A centrally located laundry closet is near both bedrooms and the full bathroom. The Carley Canyon is truly luxury apartment living designed with today's love of modern style!

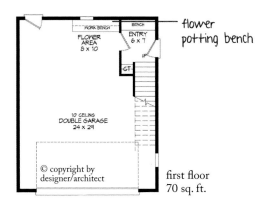

WORK BENCH BENCH
FLOWER
AREA
8 x 10
ENTRY
6 x 7
UP
GT

10' CEILINGS
DOUBLE GARAGE
24 x 29

© copyright by
designer/architect

flower
potting bench

first floor
70 sq. ft.

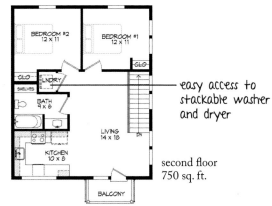

BEDROOM #2
12 x 11
BEDROOM #1
12 x 11
CLO
CLO
LNDRY
SHELVES
BATH
9 x 6
LIVING
14 x 18
DN
KITCHEN
10 x 8
BALCONY

easy access to
stackable washer
and dryer

second floor
750 sq. ft.

PLAN #C20-142D-7500

820 square feet of living area
width: 25'   depth: 34'
2 bedrooms, 1 bath
2" x 6" exterior walls
slab foundation

CUMMINGS APARTMENT GARAGE

The Cummings apartment garage is literally a vacation in your own backyard! Who said apartment garage living has to be boring? This will definitely become your hub for entertaining with both covered and uncovered amazing outdoor spaces. The first floor has a mud room with two dressing rooms, a full bath, and a kitchenette accessible from the patio, great when grilling. Upstairs, you'll find an open floor plan, one bedroom, and another full bath. This beautiful structure would also be an excellent extension off a swimming pool complete with guest space.

second floor
805 sq. ft.

DECK
45' 10" x 24' 3"

amazing
outdoor fireplace

DINING
8' 5" x 14' 4"

KITCHEN
6' 2" x 10' 0"

LIVING ROOM
20' 0" x 21' 6"

STAIR

first floor
380 sq. ft.

Upper Front
Office Space

BATH
4' 11" x 8' 0"

CLOSET

PATIO
46' 0" x 24' 4"

BEDROOM # 1
18' 0" x 14' 1"

KITCHENETTE
12' 11" x 9' 10"

MUD ROOM
15' 9" x 9' 0"

BATH
8' 5" x 6"

DRESSING   DRESSING
5' 1" x 6'   7' 1" x 6'

BATH

© copyright by
designer/architect

great mud
room with
dressing areas

2 CAR GARAGE
30' 1" x 30' 3"

STAIR

PLAN #C20-173D-7500

1185 square feet of living area
1492 bonus square feet
width: 36'   depth: 66'
1 bedroom, 2 baths
2" x 6" exterior walls
basement foundation

optional
lower level
1,492 sq. ft.

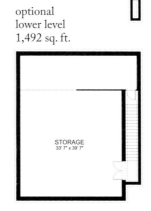

STORAGE
33' 7" x 39' 7"

JENSEN APARTMENT & RV GARAGE

Storage is literally at every turn in this two-bedroom apartment garage with space for multiple vehicles, including a recreation vehicle. A covered patio and half bath are found off the massive garage for convenience on the first floor. The second floor apartment features a kitchen with island seating for four people that overlooks the living area. Two spacious bedrooms, a bath, and tons of storage complete the space in the Jensen.

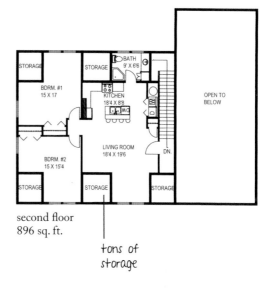

second floor
896 sq. ft.

tons of
storage

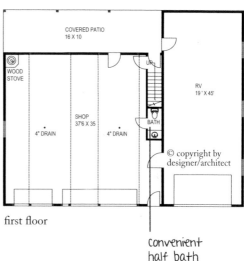

first floor

convenient
half bath

PLAN #C20-133D-7511

896 square feet of living area
width: 58' depth: 46'
2 bedrooms, 1½ baths
2" x 6" exterior walls
slab foundation

BUENA VISTA APARTMENT GARAGE

Surprise - the Buena Vista apartment garage can hold to up to three vehicles! Enter the boot room with a wrap-around bench and use it as a drop zone when arriving each day. Upstairs, you'll discover a sunny morning room greeting you at the start of each new day. The living room has a sloped ceiling making it feel more spacious. The bedroom with a nearby bath completes the interior living space, while a large balcony/deck offers great space for relaxing outdoors or entertaining when the weather is nice.

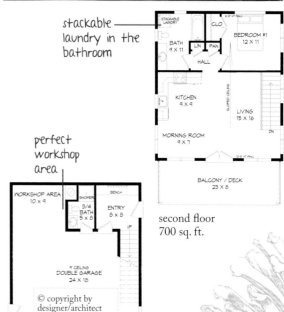

stackable laundry in the bathroom

STACKABLE LAUNDRY

CLO

BATH
9 x 11

LIN PAN

BEDROOM #1
12 X 11

HALL

KITCHEN
9 X 9

LIVING
15 X 16

SLOPED CEILING

MORNING ROOM
9 X 7

DN

BALCONY / DECK
23 X 8

second floor
700 sq. ft.

perfect workshop area

WORKSHOP AREA
10 x 9

SHOWER

3/4 BATH
5 x 8

BENCH

ENTRY
8 x 8

UP

9' CEILING
DOUBLE GARAGE
24 x 18

© copyright by
designer/architect

16' x 8' GARAGE DOOR

DECK ABOVE

first floor
131 sq. ft.

PLAN #C20-142D-7562

831 square feet of living area
width: 25'   depth: 28'
1 bedroom, 2 baths
2" x 6" exterior walls
slab foundation

WILLOW POINT APARTMENT GARAGE

Who said apartment garages have to be dull, or lack style? The Willow Point apartment garage is anything but! The modern farmhouse exterior gives way to a 3-car garage on the first floor and an open and bright living space on the second floor, with plenty of windows lining each wall for added sunlight. A roomy bedroom, a bath, and even a laundry room complete the floor plan. This style would look fantastic alongside your Modern Farmhouse home, or in a rural setting.

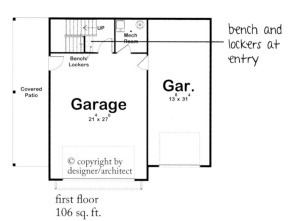

first floor
106 sq. ft.

bench and
lockers at
entry

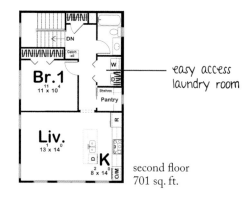

easy access
laundry room

second floor
701 sq. ft.

PLAN #C20-125D-7571

807 square feet of living area
width: 44'   depth: 35'
1 bedroom, 1 bath
slab foundation

KODY FARM

Rustic, with a rural style, the Kody Farm 4-car garage apartment has two covered carport areas and a tandem-style garage entry. The second floor has a spacious living room with fireplace, a U-shaped kitchen, two bedrooms with walk-in closets and their own baths, plus a laundry room. Small, cozy comfort!

PLAN #C20-133D-7509

1092 square feet of living area
width: 36'   depth: 50'
2 bedrooms, 2 baths
2" x 6" exterior walls
slab foundation

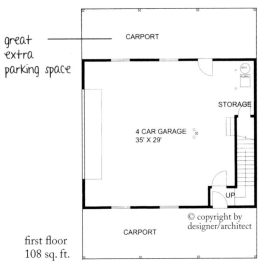

great extra parking space

CARPORT

STORAGE

4 CAR GARAGE
35' X 29'

UP

© copyright by
designer/architect

CARPORT

first floor
108 sq. ft.

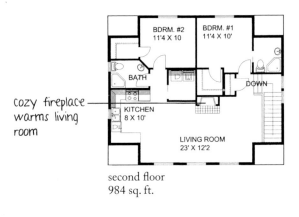

BDRM. #2
11'4 X 10'

BDRM. #1
11'4 X 10'

BATH

DOWN

KITCHEN
8 X 10'

LIVING ROOM
23' X 12'2

cozy fireplace warms living room

second floor
984 sq. ft.

JUSTINE CREEK

PLAN #C20-002D-7526

566 square feet of living area
width: 28' depth: 24'
studio, 1 bath
floating slab foundation
material list/instructions included

The charming dormers of the Justine Creek apartment garage add major curb appeal to this design. The second floor features a comfortable studio apartment with an open living area, dormer windows adding character, a corner kitchen, a walk-in closet, and a full bath.

Garage
23-5x23-4

Up

© copyright by
designer/architect

first floor

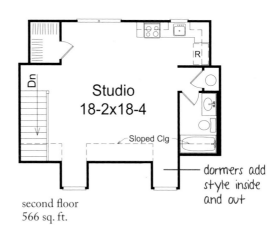

Dn

Studio
18-2x18-4

R

Sloped Clg

dormers add
style inside
and out

second floor
566 sq. ft.

PARKHILL

The Parkhill is disguised as a home but in reality offers stylish apartment garage living. The living room with dining area has a balcony deck with sliding glass door access. The kitchen has a breakfast bar, an oval window above the sink, and plenty of cabinets. The master bedroom has a walk-in closet and large window. Laundry and storage closets and mechanical space are found on the first floor.

PLAN #C20-007D-0070

929 square feet of living area
width: 31' depth: 35'
2 bedrooms, 1 bath
slab foundation

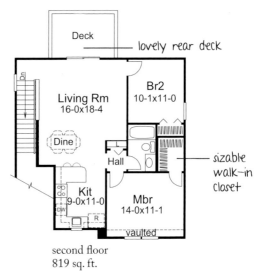

storage and laundry closet in the garage

Patio

HW F

Stor.

W
D

Garage
23-4x29-4

© copyright by designer/architect

Entry

first floor
110 sq. ft.

Porch

lovely rear deck

Deck

Living Rm
16-0x18-4

Br2
10-1x11-0

Dine

Hall

Kit
9-0x11-0

Mbr
14-0x11-1

sizable walk-in closet

vaulted

second floor
819 sq. ft.

GLENWOOD

PLAN #C20-007D-0040

632 square feet of living area
width: 28'   depth: 26'
1 bedroom, 1 bath
slab foundation

The covered porch leads to a vaulted entry featuring a staircase with an arched window, a coat closet, and access to the garage and laundry area. Upstairs in the Glenwood you'll find a cozy vaulted living room with fireplace, a large arched window, and a handy pass-through to the kitchen. There's also a luxurious bath with a garden tub and arched window above.

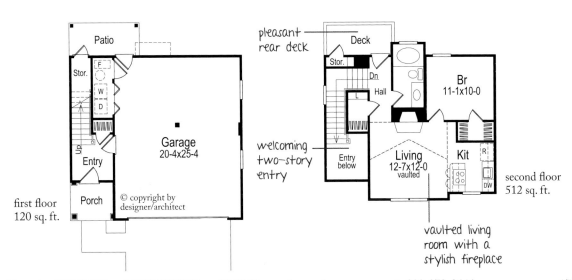

FRIDA

This sleek, vaulted studio apartment is sure to turn heads, and is a great option to complement today's ever-so popular modern home design trend. The shed-style roof of the Frida apartment garage adds eye-catching curb appeal. While the second floor studio enjoys a compact kitchen and built-in desk space, there is also a full bath with space for a stackable washer and dryer, plus a linen closet to optimize storage. Who said apartment garage living was boring?

PLAN #C20-012D-7506

336 square feet of living area
width: 17'-6"   depth: 24'
1 bedroom, 1 bath
2" x 6" exterior walls
slab foundation

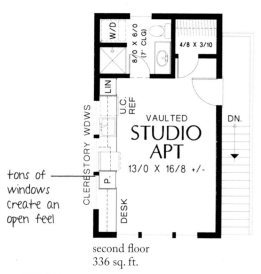

GARAGE
13/0 X 23/0

© copyright by
designer/architect

first floor

UP

W/D

8/0 X 6/0
(7' CLGI)

4/8 X 3/10

LIN

CLERESTORY WDWS

U.C.
REF

VAULTED
STUDIO
APT
13/0 X 16/8 +/-

DN.

P.

DESK

tons of
windows
create an
open feel

second floor
336 sq. ft.

PARK HOUSE

PLAN #C20-007D-0145

1005 square feet of living area
width: 40'   depth: 38'
2 bedrooms, 1½ baths
slab foundation

The Park House is a unique three-car garage with a rear apartment. This two-story apartment is disguised with a one-story facade featuring triple garage doors and a shed roof dormer. The side porch leads to an entry hall, a living room with fireplace and patio access, a U-shaped kitchen, a powder room, and a staircase to the second floor. The second floor is comprised of two bedrooms and a bath. The Park House makes the most garage apartment living.

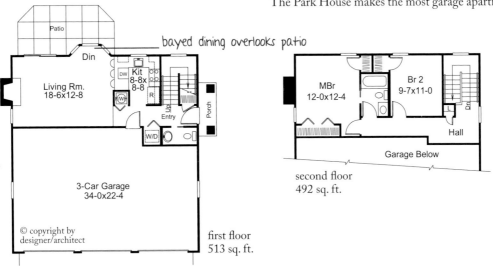

STONETRAIL
The living room has a bayed dining area, a separate entry with garage access, and a staircase to the second floor. An L-shaped kitchen has a pantry closet nearby. The second floor has a bedroom with walk-in closet. A handy RV garage is also an asset.

PLAN #C20-007D-0189
713 square feet of living area
width: 39'-4"   depth: 42'-4"
1 bedroom, 1½ baths
slab foundation

SANDON
The garage has space for a handy washer/dryer. Upstairs the second floor has a vaulted family room between the kitchen and bedroom. There is plenty of storage throughout, including built-in shelves, a closet, and a pantry.

PLAN #C20-013D-0163
838 square feet of living area
width: 42'   depth: 24'
1 bedroom, 1 bath
slab foundation standard;
basement or crawl space available for a fee

PLATEAU PARK
The beamed and vaulted great room, breakfast area, and kitchen are the main focal point of this studio apartment. A quiet bedroom and full bath complete the interior and offer great comfort.

PLAN #C20-142D-7529
780 square feet of living area
width: 30'-5"   depth: 40'
1 bedroom, 1 bath
slab foundation

SCENIC PASS
This Modern two-car apartment garage would be an ideal fit just about anywhere from the mountains to the beach. The bedroom, bath and walk-in closet are surprisingly large and luxurious.

PLAN #C20-142D-7584
793 square feet of living area
width: 33'   depth: 36'
1 bedroom, 1 bath
2" x 6" exterior walls
slab foundation

PALMERHILL
This stylish apartment garage includes plenty of storage, including built-in shelves and a desk in the living area. There is a functional U-shaped kitchen and a bedroom and bath combo, including space for a washer and dryer.

PLAN #C20-012D-7501
633 square feet of living area
width: 28'   depth: 26'
1 bedroom, 1 bath
2" x 6" exterior walls
slab foundation

PINEWOOD
The vaulted living room has a kitchenette, fireplace, and a separate entry with a closet. The staircase leads to a second floor bedroom with a bath, a walk-in closet, and a unique opening with louvered doors that can overlook the living room below.

PLAN #C20-007D-0191
641 square feet of living area
width: 28'   depth: 31'
1 bedroom, 1½ baths
slab foundation

Blueprint PRICING and ORDERING + VISIT houseplansandmore.com + 1-800-373-2646

WOLFE
This apartment garage is ideal for those who want little responsibility when they're not traveling. The layout has a kitchen, living area, and a boat/RV garage on the first floor, and a bedroom on the second floor.

PLAN #C20-108D-7509
870 square feet of living area
width: 40'   depth: 42'
1 bedroom, 1 bath
slab foundation standard;
crawl space available for a fee

CARLYN
Stylish facade with a Country French influence looks great with many styles of homes being built today. Open studio space with an L-shaped kitchen has a private bedroom down the hall.

PLAN #C20-098D-7502
540 square feet of living area
width: 40'   depth: 24'
1 bedroom, 1 bath
slab foundation

LIDA
Stately columns create a sophisticated exterior appearance loaded with curb appeal. The spacious living/dining area has a box-bay window for indoor character. The kitchen has double French doors to a second-floor deck.

PLAN #C20-071D-0246
755 square feet of living area
width: 35' depth: 30'
1 bedroom, 1 bath
2" x 6" exterior walls
slab foundation

COPPERCREEK
The Coppercreek is a 4-car apartment garage with a mud room featuring a bench and lockers on the first floor. The second floor spaces has a cathedral ceiling for spaciousness and a balcony off the bedroom.

PLAN #C20-125D-7540
1077 square feet of living area
width: 37' depth: 37'
1 bedroom, 1 bath
slab foundation

MORGAN LANE
Fashioned in Modern Farmhouse style, this apartment garage perfectly captures this distinctive style. There is more than enough space for comfortable living.

PLAN #C20-059D-7528
888 square feet of living area
width: 38'-8" depth: 34'-4"
1 bedroom, 1 bath
stem wall slab foundation

POTTS
This apartment garage can handle something as large as an RV on one end and it has an open second floor layout with a huge outdoor deck that wraps around the exterior.

PLAN #C20-173D-7505
1096 square feet of living area
width: 30'-4" depth: 60'
2 bedrooms, 2 baths
2" x 6" exterior walls
monolithic slab foundation

EDDIE
Friendly and inviting, the Eddie apartment garage has a 4-car garage on the main floor plus a separate storage garage. Upstairs, find a comfortable, open great room with L-shaped kitchen and a well-appointed bedroom and bath.

PLAN #C20-173D-7509
880 square feet of living area
width: 40'   depth: 44'
1 bedroom, 1½ baths
2" x 6" exterior walls
monolithic slab foundation

NEWTON PARK
The front entrance leads to an entry that accesses both the garage and the apartment. Located behind the garage is the perfect room for an office or workshop, and it has sliding glass doors to a rear patio so getting some fresh air is easy.

PLAN #C20-007D-0188
656 square feet of living area
width: 17'   depth: 34'
studio, 1 bath
slab foundation

Blueprint PRICING and ORDERING + VISIT houseplansandmore.com + 1-800-373-2646

HOBART
This two-car apartment garage has ample vehicle space plus an apartment with a kitchen, living and dining areas, a full bath, and a separate bedroom for plenty of privacy.

PLAN #C20-002D-7510
746 square feet of living area
width: 28'   depth: 26'
1 bedroom, 1 bath
floating slab foundation
material list/instructions included

CORTLAND BAY
So much modern curb appeal with this three-car apartment garage! The family room and kitchen form a large area with an island overlooking it all. A private bedroom is near a bath for ease.

PLAN #C20-125D-7541
932 square feet of living area
width: 47'   depth: 40'
1 bedroom, 1 bath
slab foundation

WHITNEY HILL GARAGE WITH LOFT

The Whitney Hill workshop garage is a convenient two-car garage with a workshop and a partial loft space above, ideal for storage. A large workshop on the main floor has a 6' x 6'-8" double door, allowing easy entry into the space when working on mechanics or larger items or machinery. The addition of the partial loft offers extra storage, always appreciated by hobby enthusiasts.

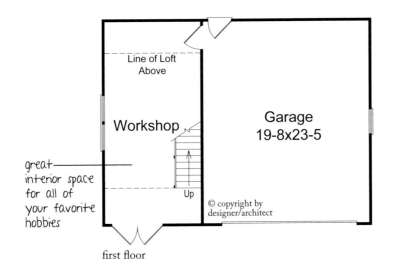

Line of Loft Above

Workshop

Garage
19-8x23-5

great interior space for all of your favorite hobbies

Up

© copyright by designer/architect

first floor

Knee Wall Height at 4'-0"

Dn

Loft Ceiling Height at 7'-10"

Knee Wall Height at 4'-0"

second floor
190 sq. ft.

PLAN #C20-002D-6002

190 bonus square feet
width: 32' depth: 24'
building height: 20'-2"
floating slab foundation
material list/instructions included

BIGLEY GARAGE WITH LOFT

This two-car garage is a wonderful structure that adds so much character to any backyard or lot. Not only is it an attractive way to house additional vehicles, yard equipment, and other items, it has a classic look that looks great with many architectural styles of homes. If you need an additional garage or storage spot, then look no further than the charming Bigley garage with loft above.

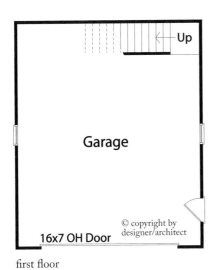

Garage

← Up

16x7 OH Door

© copyright by
designer/architect

first floor

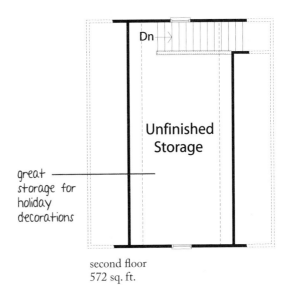

Dn →

Unfinished
Storage

great
storage for
holiday
decorations

second floor
572 sq. ft.

PLAN #C20-059D-6107

572 bonus square feet
width: 22'   depth: 26'
building height: 23'-8"
footing and foundation wall foundation

LIBBY COVE GARAGE WITH LOFT

This two-car garage with large loft above has so much to offer! Off the garage is a rear covered porch for enjoying a much-appreciated shaded outdoor space. The second-floor loft has multiple windows creating a simple Craftsman appearance to the exterior. There is the option to add a half bath, and there is double door access onto a huge deck with a spiral staircase leading to the ground floor. An ultra private third-floor deck is the perfect private sunning spot.

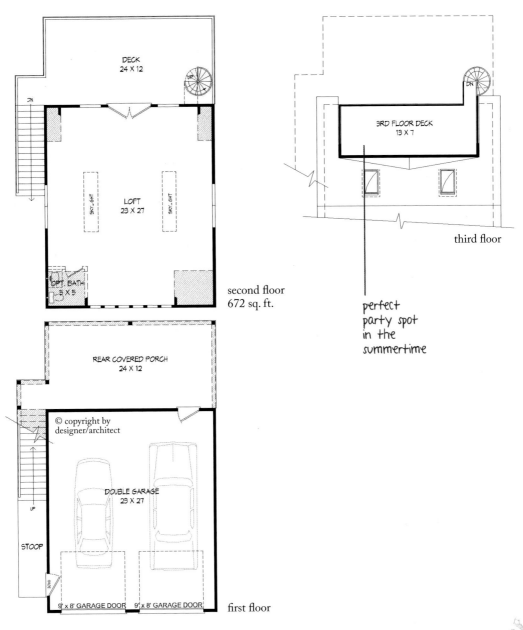

DECK
24 X 12

UP

DN

LOFT
23 X 27

SKY LGHT

SKY LGHT

OPT. BATH
5 X 5

second floor
672 sq. ft.

3RD FLOOR DECK
13 X 7

DN

third floor

perfect
party spot
in the
summertime

REAR COVERED PORCH
24 X 12

© copyright by
designer/architect

DOUBLE GARAGE
23 X 27

UP

STOOP

9' x 8' GARAGE DOOR

9' x 8' GARAGE DOOR

first floor

PLAN #C20-142D-6135

672 bonus square feet
width: 28'   depth: 40'
$^1/_2$ bath
building height: 26'-7"
slab foundation

SOMMERTON

The Sommerton garage has a shingle-style roof and a large dormer window, adding style to the exterior of this two-car garage structure with a workshop and storage. A quaint covered front porch offers a great place for taking a break from a tedious project. The workshop includes ladder access to the storage loft above.

PLAN #C20-117D-6000

1058 bonus square feet
width: 30'   depth: 25'
building height: 24'
2" x 6" exterior walls
slab foundation

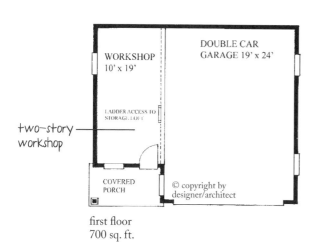

two-story workshop

WORKSHOP 10' x 19'

DOUBLE CAR GARAGE 19' x 24'

LADDER ACCESS TO STORAGE LOFT

COVERED PORCH

© copyright by designer/architect

first floor
700 sq. ft.

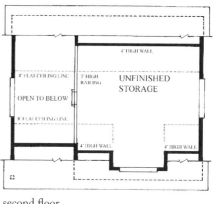

4' HIGH WALL

8' FLAT CEILING LINE

3' HIGH RAILING

UNFINISHED STORAGE

OPEN TO BELOW

8' FLAT CEILING LINE

4' HIGH WALL

4' HIGH WALL

second floor
358 sq. ft.

LANELLE

PLAN #C20-059D-6013

527 bonus square feet
width: 32'   depth: 26'
building height: 26'
footing and foundation wall foundation

Undeniable charm plays a huge part in the style of the Lanelle two-car garage with a trio of dormer windows. The windows fill the unfinished storage area with plenty of natural light, making it a cheerful workshop or home office space.

second floor
527 sq. ft.

windows
add light to
storage

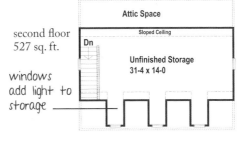

first floor
832 sq. ft.

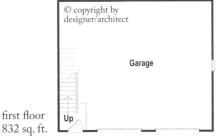

The Adkins two-car garage with an easy-to-access shop is the ideal option for your backyard. Designed with a nod to Modern Farmhouse style, the shop has its own covered entrance and features a built-in workbench for making projects a cinch to complete.

PLAN #C20-125D-6091

788 bonus square feet
width: 34'   depth: 26'
building height: 21'
slab foundation

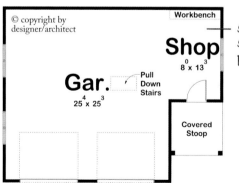

© copyright by designer/architect

Workbench

Shop
8 x 13³⁰

Gar.
25⁴ x 25³

Pull Down Stairs

Covered Stoop

spacious shop with separate covered porch entry

HOMESTEAD

PLAN #C20-117D-6001

458 bonus square feet
width: 24'   depth: 35'
building height: 23'
2" x 6" exterior walls
slab foundation

The lovely Homestead rustic Craftsman two-car garage features an open two-story entry and workshop space with a coat closet. The open second floor is perfect for storage, a spacious art studio, or hobby room, and it has three large windows filling the space with plenty of natural sunlight.

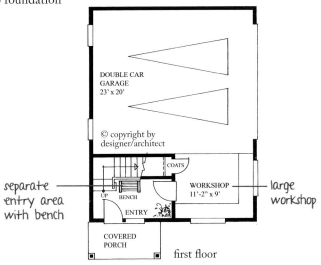

separate entry area with bench

large workshop

DOUBLE CAR GARAGE
23' x 20'

© copyright by designer/architect

COATS

WORKSHOP
11'-2" x 9'

UP   BENCH

ENTRY

COVERED PORCH

first floor

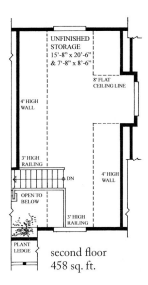

UNFINISHED STORAGE
15'-8" x 20'-6"
& 7'-8" x 8'-6"

8' FLAT CEILING LINE

4' HIGH WALL

3' HIGH RAILING

DN

4' HIGH WALL

OPEN TO BELOW

3' HIGH RAILING

PLANT LEDGE

second floor
458 sq. ft.

The Hector garage with loft features space for three vehicles and has a rustic Craftsman-influenced facade, great with many of today's home designs. The second-floor loft space includes a cozy wood stove for added warmth when working on projects in the cooler months of the year.

PLAN #C20-126D-1056

384 bonus square feet
width: 30'   depth: 24'
building height: 23'
2" x 6" exterior walls
basement foundation

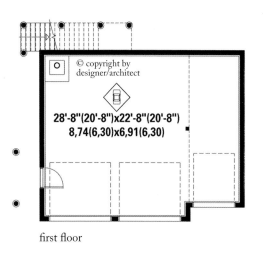

© copyright by
designer/architect

28'-8"(20'-8")x22'-8"(20'-8")
8,74(6,30)x6,91(6,30)

first floor

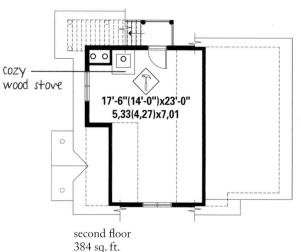

cozy
wood stove

17'-6"(14'-0")x23'-0"
5,33(4,27)x7,01

second floor
384 sq. ft.

SAVANNA

PLAN #C20-142D-7510

1027 bonus square feet
width: 24'-10"   depth: 32'-10"
building height: 27'-8"
1 bath
slab foundation

A garage with many purposes! The Savanna single-car garage has a large office on the first floor in addition to a full bath with a walk-in shower. Plenty of additional storage is found near the garage, making this space also ideal as a workshop. The second floor is an open recreation room space, perfect as a man cave or a family game room.

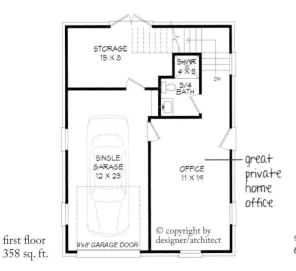

STORAGE
15 X 8

SH/WR
4 X 8

3/4
BATH

DN

SINGLE
GARAGE
12 X 23

OFFICE
11 X 19

great private home office

© copyright by designer/architect

9'x8' GARAGE DOOR

first floor
358 sq. ft.

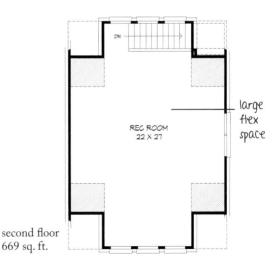

DN

REC ROOM
22 X 27

large flex space

second floor
669 sq. ft.

MAYER LANE

The charming style of the Mayer Lane two-car loft garage is so appealing it will be a welcome addition to any backyard and also looks great with many architectural styles of homes. Windows on all four walls of the second-floor attic add sunlight to the interior, making it a very functional space that's cheerful enough for a home office.

PLAN #C20-136D-6001

590 bonus square feet
width: 26'   depth: 28'
building height: 25'-3"
slab foundation

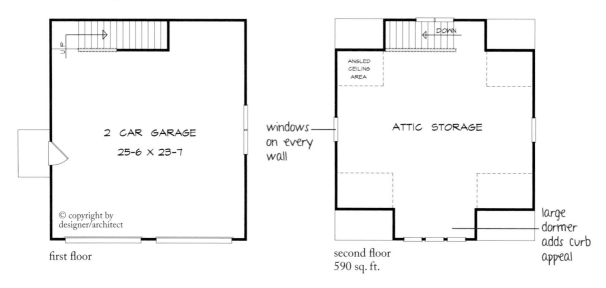

UP

2 CAR GARAGE
25-6 X 23-7

© copyright by designer/architect

first floor

windows on every wall

DOWN

ANGLED CEILING AREA

ATTIC STORAGE

large dormer adds curb appeal

second floor
590 sq. ft.

WATERVILLE

PLAN #C20-012D-7500

1179 bonus square feet
width: 48'   depth: 36'
1 bath
building height: 25'-6"
2" x 6" exterior walls
slab foundation

The Waterville garage and loft offers three garage bays, a large storage area, and a full bath on the first floor. The vaulted second floor bonus room would make an ideal home office or hobby area and includes an outdoor balcony to get a much needed break and some fresh air every now and then.

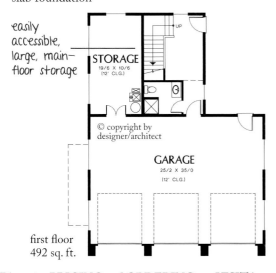

easily accessible, large, main-floor storage

STORAGE
19/6 X 10/6
(12" CLG.)

© copyright by designer/architect

GARAGE
25/2 X 35/0
(12" CLG.)

first floor
492 sq. ft.

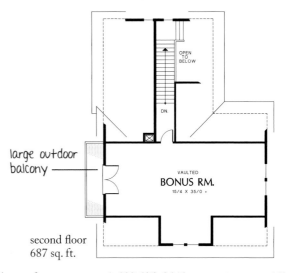

OPEN TO BELOW

DN.

large outdoor balcony

VAULTED
BONUS RM.
15/4 X 35/0 +

second floor
687 sq. ft.

RICHERT

This two-car garage makes a great addition to any lot that features a country-style barn or shed. It includes two large garage bays and storage overhead, all with a clean, simple style.

PLAN #C20-059D-6076

171 bonus square feet
width: 34' depth: 27'
building height: 24'
footing and foundation wall foundation

KARISMA

Sit in the shade of the covered porch and enjoy this perfect entertaining or relaxing spot. Two large storage spaces on the second floor can also convert to living spaces, such as a home office or artist's studio.

PLAN #C20-108D-6000

664 bonus square feet
width: 38' depth: 24'
building height: 24'-8"
2" x 6" exterior walls
slab foundation standard;
basement or crawl space available for a fee

HILLER POINT

This garage with loft has two garage bays for cars or smaller vehicles, and another for an RV. You'll easily be able to house all of your motorized vehicles in this roomy garage.

PLAN #C20-171D-6017

627 bonus square feet
width: 34'-4" depth: 28'
building height: 19'
2" x 6" exterior walls
concrete block foundation

TARYN

The perfect two-car garage with loft option for any classic Country, Traditional, or Cape Cod style home. Twin dormers add additional sunlight to the second-story loft and an undeniable charm all their own.

PLAN #C20-002D-6001

599 bonus square feet
width: 28' depth: 24'
building height: 21'
slab foundation
material list/instructions included

ALISSA
This stylish two-car garage has storage space on the main floor making it easy to access through a side garage door. Whether it's patio furniture, an ATV, or kid's bicycles, easily stow away seasonal items in style.

PLAN #C20-113D-6039
464 bonus square feet
width: 22' depth: 44'
building height: 15'-8"
2" x 6" exterior walls
floating slab or monolithic slab foundation, please specify when ordering

GARNET HILL
This charming garage features a first floor workshop, and a second floor hobby room, perfect for crafters and DIYers, or turn this sun-filled space into a perfect private home office.

PLAN #C20-136D-6009
600 bonus square feet
width: 32' depth: 28'
building height: 28'-10"
2" x 6" exterior walls
slab foundation

DUTCH HAVEN
This 3-car garage with loft has a handy half bath and plenty of space for an overflow storage space. Its shingle siding, Craftsman details and European charm make it a stunner in any backyard.

PLAN #C20-168D-6000
845 bonus square feet
width: 38' depth: 32'-6"
building height: 25'-9"
1/2 bath
slab foundation

STAPLETON HILL
Shake siding accents on the exterior make a lasting impression with this two-car garage with roomy loft above. Wouldn't a hobby or craft room be ideal in this attractive garage?

PLAN #C20-125D-6044
1104 bonus square feet
width: 24' depth: 26'
building height: 23'
slab foundation

MONARCH BEND
A stylish two-car garage with storage or game room space on the second floor. Make this your teenager's spot to retreat to, or a man cave game room for boy's poker night.

PLAN #C20-171D-7500
498 bonus square feet
width: 37'   depth: 26'
building height: 23'
2" x 6" exterior walls
concrete block foundation

WHITELY
Roomy one-car garage has a second floor loft and a first floor workshop with a sink and a warming wood stove. It has plenty of extra space for an ATV, bicycles or other outdoor recreational gear.

PLAN #C20-113D-6044
442 bonus square feet
width: 34'   depth: 26'
building height: 19'-7"
2" x 6" exterior walls
floating slab or monolithic slab foundation, please specify when ordering

WINSTON LANE
This two-car garage has a second-floor loft providing extra storage, while the clerestory window brightens the interior, eliminating the need and expense of installing electricity if you desire.

PLAN #C20-171D-6006
500 bonus square feet
width: 26'   depth: 25'
building height: 23'
2" x 6" exterior walls
slab foundation

CLOVER CREEK
This attractive two-car garage with loft has an interior staircase for accessing the second floor easily, and its classic good looks will complement many architectural styles.

PLAN #C20-171D-6010
570 bonus square feet
width: 28'   depth: 26'
building height: 26'
2" x 6" exterior walls
concrete block foundation

TIARA
Classic country-style two-car garage has a staircase leading to the storage space overhead and is an ideal design for keeping your home uncluttered and organized.

PLAN #C20-002D-6039
540 bonus square feet
width: 28'   depth: 24'
building height: 21'
floating slab foundation
material list included

SHERRY HILL
This classic barn-style one-car garage offer a large storage space on the main floor for convenience and a covered side porch, ideal for just relaxing in the shade and watching the kid's play outdoors.

PLAN #C20-173D-6016
495 bonus square feet
width: 21'   depth: 29'
building height: 18'-6"
monolithic slab foundation

SONOMA BAY
Designed with a nod to the Modern Farmhouse style, this two-car garage has a side porch, a full bath, workshop and dog trot on the first floor and a vaulted workshop and bonus area on the second floor. Stylish and functional!

PLAN #C20-142D-7601
767 bonus square feet
width: 36'   depth: 42'-6"
building height: 30'
1 bath
2" x 6" exterior walls
slab foundation

NAPLES SHORE
The Naples Shore two-car garage with studio loft space above has a unique slant roof that goes from 6' to 11' on the second floor, creating quite a dramatic space for an art studio or inspired office.

PLAN #C20-142D-6116
720 bonus square feet
width: 30'   depth: 24'
building height: 21'-5"
2" x 6" exterior walls
slab foundation

BEFORE BUILDING A SHED OR SMALL STRUCTURE

Building a shed or another small structure can be a simple project if the proper planning and guidelines are followed. Now more often than ever, people are turning to do-it-yourself projects as a way of adding additional storage, creating a place to enjoy hobbies and pastimes, or providing an entertainment or relaxation space, or even a home office. Why not build a shed or smaller structure to satisfy your specific needs?

A shed or other small structure, such as a studio, guest quarters, home office, or workshop, can potentially increase the value of your property while maintaining a well-organized home with the space you originally started with. Plus, the additional space will allow your household to run smoother. Maybe your family needs a workshop, or perhaps you need a utility shed for yard or garden equipment. Whatever your needs, there are hundreds of great sheds and other smaller structures designed to provide the perfect function you seem to be missing with your current home situation.

Here are some important factors to consider when constructing projects such as these to build on your existing lot. Before selecting a plan, review this checklist of design information you should gather before you make a final decision.

LOCAL BUILDING REQUIREMENTS

Visit your local building department and determine how local building codes and zoning ordinances will influence your project. Are you able to build a separate structure from your existing home? Are there height and size restrictions?

DEED RESTRICTIONS

Are there conditions in your property deed that restrict the type and location of an additional structure? Are you planning to place your shed or building on property controlled by an existing easement or utility access?

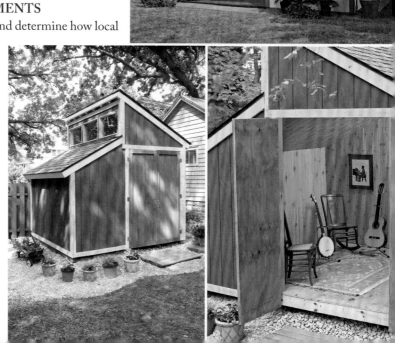

CLIMATIC FACTORS

Evaluate the micro-climate of your intended structure location. Micro-climate includes the shading effects of trees and shrubs, the angle of the sun in relation to nearby landscaping during different seasons, soil drainage conditions, and prevailing wind and temperature conditions. Remember, an enclosed shed without temperature regulation needs to be protected from the sun in the summer and exposed to any available sunlight in the winter, otherwise it will be impossible to use due to its comfort level.

OVERALL FUNCTION

Remember, the structure you intend to build should not only be functional, but should be an attractive addition to your yard. It can make a wonderful place for a gardener to house their tools and supplies, or create a workshop or hobby area perfectly designed for you and your needs. Adding storage shelves, electricity, and other amenities can only make your shed more personalized and functional to your needs. Always keep in mind the architectural style of your home on the land and do your best to complement your new structure to your existing home for a seamless and thoughtful finished look.

CHOOSING LUMBER FOR YOUR SHED

It is also important to think about what kind of lumber best suits your shed or structure. Consider both the positive and negative attributes of various lumber types. Below is a concise guide to some common softwood lumber species used in construction. As you will see, each type of wood has its own good and bad qualities. You may make your decision based on your region of the country, the wood most commonly used in your area, or its durability. You may have a deck or other structure in your backyard already built with a specific type of wood. You may decide to use the same type for consistency.

- Cedar, Western Red - Popular for the durability and decay-resistance of its heartwood.
- Cypress - Cypress resists decay, is an attractive reddish coloration, and holds paint well.
- Douglas Fir, Larch - Douglas fir has great strength and is used best in the framing of your shed, especially in the floor joist members.
- Pines - Numerous pine species have excellent workability but are often pressure-treated for use in exterior construction.
- Southern Pine - Unlike the soft pines described above, southern pines possess strength but are only moderately decay and warp resistant.
- Poplar - Poplar has moderate strength and resists decay and warping.
- Redwood - A premium construction material because of its durability, resistance to decay, and beautiful natural brownish-red coloration.

A shed, studio, or other structure will not only provide necessary shelter and storage space, it can potentially increase the value of your home, making it a worthwhile addition, financially as well as for better function. Browse through our stylish sheds and other great small structures and find the perfect design for your specific needs.

SMALL STRUCTURES

Plan #C20-117D-6002 found on page 208.

All types of small structures can provide storage flexibility, ways to create additional income, or extra square footage to create better function in your existing home and life. Architects and designers now more than ever understand the needs of homeowners and are designing amazing small structures of all kinds that enhance your ability to relax, help you create space for hobbies, rid you of clutter, provide a productive work environment, or allow you to create comfortable spaces for loved ones or possibly renters. The options are endless when creating a space that is comfortable, fulfilling, and possibly even profitable. Whatever it is that you are searching for, there is a small structure perfect for you.

RABURN
POOL HOUSE

Enjoy entertaining to the fullest in the Raburn pool house. Step out of the sun just in time to avoid that burn and cool off in style in the sleek confines of this cool pool house bungalow. With its overhead garage style door, simply lift the door above and enjoy a light breeze as it enters the entire shaded space. It's the perfect way to enjoy warmer days poolside and entertain in total comfort and style. Or, wait until the sun goes down, shake up a cocktail at happy hour and relax in luxury in the posh setting of the Raburn pool house.

handy half bath

© copyright by
designer/architect

21⁴ x 14⁴

garage style
overhead door

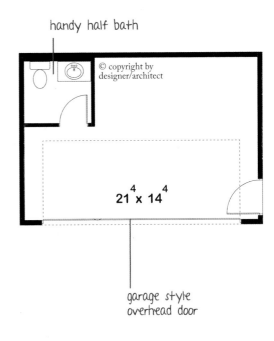

PLAN #C20-125D-7502

330 square feet of living area
width: 21'-4"   depth: 14'-4"
building height: 12'
1 half bath
slab foundation

ROGERS RV GARAGE & WORKSHOP

The Rogers RV garage and workshop could be the perfect combination of fun and function for a retiree or hobby enthusiast! Store your recreational vehicle when not in use, and also enjoy tinkering with your favorite hobbies in an organized, designated place you can call your own. The workshop offers a tremendous amount of counterspace that wraps the entire space, perfect for organizing auto parts or hobby supplies.

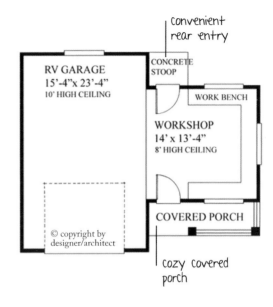

convenient rear entry

RV GARAGE
15'-4"x 23'-4"
10' HIGH CEILING

CONCRETE STOOP

WORK BENCH

WORKSHOP
14' x 13'-4"
8' HIGH CEILING

© copyright by designer/architect

COVERED PORCH

cozy covered porch

PLAN #C20-117D-6002

580 square feet of living area
width: 30'   depth: 24'
building height: 19'-6"
slab foundation

Zoom meetings and emails just got a little more tolerable thanks to the Julian Bay office. Channel your island vibes while working on this month's spreadsheet and when it's time for a break, just grab your board for a quick pick-me-up in the salty surf. The soothing interior makes the Julian Bay a tranquil place for inspiration, whether you're a writer, artist or innovative entrepreneur, this atmosphere provides a place for creative thoughts to easily come to fruition all day long! It would make working from home almost feel like a vacation!

210

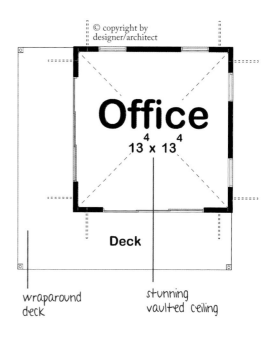

© copyright by
designer/architect

Office
13 x 13⁴

Deck

wraparound
deck

stunning
vaulted ceiling

PLAN #C20-125D-7562

196 square feet of living area
width: 14'   depth: 14'
building height: 14'
slab foundation

CASSELL CLUBHOUSE

Build your very own clubhouse and create a special place where the whole family can relax and enjoy time together! The billiard room easily becomes a game hub for all of your family's favorite activities. It connects to a rear covered porch, perfect for a barbecue grill. There are also large men's and women's bathrooms, featuring multiple toilets and showers, making this a great option poolside or as an entertaining space.

PLAN #C20-075D-7506

691 square feet of living area
width: 35'-5"   depth: 27'
2 baths
slab foundation

Blueprint PRICING and ORDERING + VISIT houseplansandmore.com + 1-800-373-2646

MARISELA GAME ROOM

PLAN #C20-009D-7542

780 square feet of living area
width: 28'   depth: 37'-9"
1 bath
building height: 15'-6"
slab foundation

The front covered patio is perfect for a hot tub or lounge area and accesses a sauna and full bath. The open room is designed for billiards or parties and has a corner fireplace, a 10' walk-in bar with storage, and space for darts, a jukebox, a popcorn machine, or pinball machine, making this a hub for family fun!

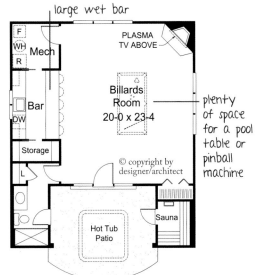

large wet bar

F
WH
R
Mech

PLASMA
TV ABOVE

Bar

DW

Billards
Room
20-0 x 23-4

Storage

plenty
of space
for a pool
table or
pinball
machine

L

© copyright by
designer/architect

Hot Tub
Patio

Sauna

CABANA COOL POOL HOUSE

Have it made in the shade of the Cabana Cool pool house! Take a break in the summertime from the heat of the day and enjoy an iced cold beverage, or when a chill begins to fill the air, curl up next to the roaring stone fireplace and enjoy the cooler temps with a cup of warm cider and a good book. This welcome retreat will be inviting all year long.

PLAN #C20-175D-7505

400 square feet of living area
width: 20'   depth: 25'
building height: 17'-2"
2" x 6" exterior walls
slab foundation

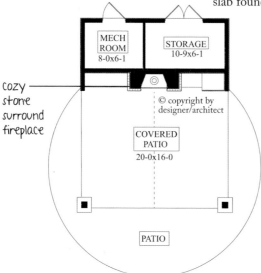

MECH ROOM
8-0x6-1

STORAGE
10-9x6-1

cozy stone surround fireplace

© copyright by designer/architect

COVERED PATIO
20-0x16-0

PATIO

ROGAN COVE FLEX SPACE

PLAN #C20-125D-7566

384 square feet of living area
width: 16'   depth: 32'
2" x 6" exterior walls
building height: 14'
slab foundation

The Rogan Cove is a modern flex shelter that would make a great addition to any backyard. Whether you're in need of a private office space, or you're looking for a studio style exercise or yoga experience, this attractive modern structure has storage, a half bath and plenty of floor space for work or play.

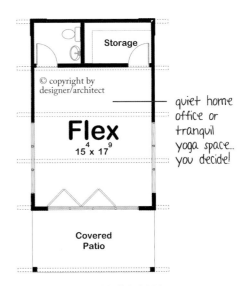

Storage

© copyright by designer/architect

Flex
15 x 17

quiet home office or tranquil yoga space... you decide!

Covered Patio

HAMMEL STUDIO

The Hammel office studio has a sleek modern style everyone today loves. With a covered patio, a full bath with a walk-in shower, a kitchenette, and a spot for a stackable washer and dryer, this structure can easily convert to a stylish studio apartment or provide multiple functions with no problem.

PLAN #C20-011D-0603

312 square feet of living area
width: 26'   depth: 12'
1 bedroom, 1 bath
building height: 10'-6"
2" x 6" exterior walls
crawl space or slab foundation standard; basement available for a fee

OFFICE / STUDIO
16/6 X 11/4
(8' CLG)

FOLD'G WALL HUNG TABLE

W D

OPEN SHLVS

© copyright by designer/architect

efficient kitchen

PATIO

large covered patio

ELLENDALE PAVILION

PLAN #C20-009D-7530

814 square feet of living area
width: 24'   depth: 47'
1 bath
building height: 15'-6"
slab foundation

A vaulted ceiling with skylights, a hot tub, a kitchen/bar, a sauna room, and a full bath highlight this design. Located at the rear is a 24' x 12' covered vaulted patio with outdoor fireplace and optional skylights. Add an outdoor grill and you have an exceptional party space or poolside structure.

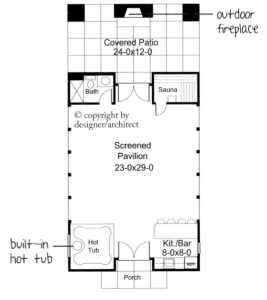

outdoor fireplace

Covered Patio
24-0x12-0

Bath

Sauna

© copyright by designer/architect

Screened Pavilion
23-0x29-0

built-in hot tub

Hot Tub

Kit./Bar
8-0x8-0

Porch

SUMMERVILLE
A bath and an open bar featuring a designated wall for a TV are conveniently located on the porch and patio of this adorable poolside cabana. Take a seat, grab a drink, and enjoy life!

PLAN #C20-009D-7524
112 square feet of living area
width: 22'   depth: 24'
1 bath
building height: 16'-6"
slab foundation

WESLAN
For those of you who can't tear away from your favorite hobbies and home projects, this workshop includes a full bath and plenty of space for those late nights when you decide to crash on the couch.

PLAN #C20-142D-4503
450 square feet of living area
width: 15'   depth: 30'
1 bath
building height: 13'-6"
slab foundation

AURORA PEAK
An outdoor lodge getaway has a vaulted interior with rustic beams and a cozy fireplace. There's a large outdoor deck, perfect for grilling, dining, or sunning. A perfect après skiing spot to relax.

PLAN #C20-142D-7506
306 square feet of living area
width: 22'-6"   depth: 21'
building height: 16'-5"
slab foundation

AVA LAGO
A perfect poolside structure to entice family members to come outside and stay awhile. The vaulted cabana has a wet bar and lanai, plus a half bath, barn door-style TV cabinet, and storage area.

PLAN #C20-142D-7555
586 square feet of living area
width: 24'   depth: 24'
1/2 bath
building height: 16'-9"
slab foundation

CABANA COVE
Take entertaining to a whole new level with this poolside structure, featuring an activity room, an island kitchen, a bedroom, bath, and covered porch with a cozy outdoor fireplace.

PLAN #C20-055D-1029
1117 square feet of living area
width: 62'   depth: 50'-6"
1 bedroom, 1 bath
building height: 24'
crawl space or slab foundation,
please specify when ordering

JUNO COVE
This modern-style cabana features an outdoor kitchen with a built-in grill and seating for four at the island. A separate storage space keeps everything organized when hosting a backyard bash.

PLAN #C20-174D-7501
240 square feet of living area
width: 20'   depth: 12'
building height: 12'
slab foundation

BAR HOP
The Bar Hop is an ideal backyard structure featuring an outdoor kitchen, rec room with garage door, a half bath, laundry room, and a studio apartment with a full bath and patio access.

PLAN #C20-175D-7506
744 square feet of living area
width: 51'   depth: 34'
1 bedroom, 1 ½ baths
building height: 19'-9"
slab foundation

LONG
A modern studio that looks perfect with the ever-popular Modern Farmhouse architecture style. Plenty of storage and a full bath with an oversized shower make this a very versatile choice as in-law quarters, too.

PLAN #C20-165D-7500
480 square feet of living area
width: 30'   depth: 16'
1 bath
building height: 13'-2"
slab foundation

CHESTERFIELD HILL This

structure would make a nice hunting cabin on acreage. With a lovely covered porch, it also has a refrigerator and sink for supplies and food and a built-in gun cabinet.

PLAN #C20-125D-4517

192 square feet of living area
width: 16'   depth: 16'
building height: 13'-3"
slab foundation

DESTINY This music studio can also easily be

used as a guest house. Inside you'll find a vaulted control room with kitchenette, a separate foyer for privacy, a half bath, and a insulated sound room that could be a comfortable bedroom.

PLAN #C20-142D-7522

413 square feet of living area
width: 22'   depth: 18'-9"
$1/2$ bath
building height: 13'-6"
slab foundation

Blueprint PRICING and ORDERING + VISIT houseplansandmore.com + 1-800-373-2646

MOORPARK A side-gabled structure

featuring 2" x 6" walls, a vaulted living area that can also be used for sleeping space. Space-saving table design, a wardrobe closet, kitchenette, and bath complete the layout.

PLAN #C20-012D-7507

322 square feet of living area
width: 14'   depth: 23'
1 bedroom, 1 bath
crawl space or slab standard;
basement available for a fee

MAXWELL HILL Let the fun begin

at the Maxwell Hill bar with loft above. A covered patio with a cathedral ceiling looks over a bar top with a sink and two built-in refrigerators. A loft above is a great retreat.

PLAN #C20-125D-7513

224 square feet of living area
width: 14'   depth: 16'
building height: 20'
slab foundation

OLSEN
The Olsen Pavilion takes shaded outdoor relaxation space to a whole new level thanks to its stunning fireplace, chandelier and overhead can lighting. The perfect place to unwind for your yard or poolside with grill space, and even a roomy storage space.

PLAN #C20-173D-7504
621 square feet of living area
width: 18' depth: 34'
building height: 16'-9"
monolithic slab foundation

SHADEWELL
Be comfortable year-round in the Shadewell cabana. With the stone fireplace, this outdoor space will be comfortable even in the winter. Grab a cold one from the bar/grill and relax in the vaulted lanai with a TV cabinet behind barn doors. A half bath, walk-in pantry and storage complete the structure.

PLAN #C20-142D-7598
777 square feet of living area
width: 32' depth: 24'
building height: 17'-1"
1/2 bath
slab foundation

WATERSHED
The perfect shaded cabana for your pool or yard! There's a roomy bath with benches for getting ready after a dip in the pool. The vaulted lanai and bar/grill offer plenty of space to party in style.

PLAN #C20-142D-7595
384 square feet of living area
width: 24' depth: 16'
1 bath
building height: 17'
slab foundation

MILES BEACH
This cabana features an outdoor kitchen with grill, a range, refrigerator, and a sink for easy outdoor entertaining. The interior has an open space with a kitchenette, a large bath, and a bedroom.

PLAN #C20-113D-7508
360 square feet of living area
width: 28' depth: 20'
1 bedroom, 1 bath
building height: 14'-4"
monolithic slab standard;
crawl space or floating slab available for a fee

MORROW

The vaulted interior creates openness that's appreciated in this small footprint. The living area doubles as sleeping space, or make this an ideal in-law suite. There's a fold-down space-saving table for mealtime, a kitchenette, and a bath with a walk-in shower.

PLAN #C20-012D-7508

322 square feet of living area
width: 14'   depth: 23'
1 bath
2" x 6" exterior walls
crawl space or slab standard;
basement available for a fee

KELLIANNE

This could be the perfect office, thanks to an entry closet, an extra storage closet, a toilet room, and a staircase to a basement storm shelter providing additional function.

PLAN #C20-009D-7507

350 square feet of living area
width: 24'   depth: 36'
1 bedroom, $^1/_2$ bath
building height: 18'
basement foundation

CHANDLER LANE

This clever structure is part garage, but it also creates an ideal spot for an outdoor kitchen and grill under a covered side porch. It can also shield garbage receptacles from the weather.

PLAN #C20-032D-1005

384 square feet of living area
width: 16'   depth: 24'
building height: 13'-8"
2" x 6" exterior walls
floating slab or monolithic slab foundation,
please specify when ordering

CAREFREE

This studio pool house is open and perfect for stepping out of the sun and cooling off. It could also be used as guest or in-law quarters since it has a full bath and a large storage closet.

PLAN #C20-142D-7520

385 square feet of living area
width: 18'   depth: 24'
1 bath
building height: 14'-6"
concrete block exterior walls
slab foundation

TINLEY
A great design for weekend fun! This would be ideal as a fishing/hunting camp. There's an insulated bunk room and a vaulted screened porch that keeps insects out while still allowing a breeze to flow through. Find plenty of storage under the bunk room.

PLAN #C20-124D-7500
192 square feet of living area
width: 12' depth: 16'
1 bedroom
building height: 11'-4"
crawl space foundation

MIRAGE
This modern cabana cottage would be amazing as guest quarters or when entertaining poolside. It includes an open island kitchen, a fireplace, space for a stackable washer/dryer, two bedrooms, a bath, and a covered porch ideal for an outdoor kitchen.

PLAN #C20-126D-1153
776 square feet of living area
width: 40' depth: 26'
2 bedrooms, 1 bath
building height: 21'
2" x 6" exterior walls
slab foundation

SUMMERSUN
This fun pool pavilion has a walk-up bar, a sauna room, and a full bath with two storage rooms to the rear. Create memories all summer around your pool or patio with this fun place!

PLAN #C20-009D-7527
151 square feet of living area
width: 26' depth: 17'
1 bath
building height: 13'
slab foundation

VINCE
This is a the perfect place to relax while the kids play, and the multiple windows allow for great views from every side so you can always keep your eye on them when they head outdoors.

PLAN #C20-124D-7501
192 square feet of living area
width: 12' depth: 16'
building height: 11'-4"
crawl space foundation

SHEDS

Whether you're a gardening enthusiast looking for some additional space or the family handyman longing for a workshop or hobby storage area, this selection of sheds will be ideal for so many different needs. Browse through this selection and then order online, or find countless more shed plans at houseplansandmore.com.

KORBIN
The classic look of this barn-style shed is a great country-style accessory for your yard. The covered side porch offers dry storage for firewood and other items, guarding them from the elements.

PLAN #C20-160D-4500
168 square feet
width: 19'   depth: 14'
building height: 16'
raised wood floor or slab foundation,
please specify when ordering

MAXINE
This attractive shed has clerestory windows for added light. With an interior rear wall height of 7'-3" and a 5' x 6'-9" double-door, this shed is easy to access.

PLAN #C20-002D-4515
includes 3 sizes:
10' x 10'   12' x 10'   14' x 10'
building height: 10'-11"
wood floor on 4x6 runners foundation
material list/instructions included

MONACA
The perfect option for garden storage that offers a convenient double-entry door for storing gardening supplies and tools easily.

PLAN #C20-002D-4519
80 square feet
width: 10'   depth: 8'
building height: 9'-6"
wood floor on 4x4 runners foundation
material list/instructions included

DOMANI
This sleek modern-style shed makes additional storage far from an eyesore. Built-in windows add daylight, making it easy to locate its contents, and the style is a great backyard focal point.

PLAN #C20-127D-4514
9 sizes available:
12'x8'   12'x10'   12'x12'
14'x8'   14'x10'   14'x12'
16'x8'   16'x10'   16'x12'
wood floor on concrete block foundation
construction prints are 8$\frac{1}{2}$" x 11"

MONESSEN
This shed offers complete flexibility since it can be built to be as big as 16' x 8' or as small as 8' x 8', whatever works best for your needs and your lot size. Total flexibility is a great feature!

PLAN #C20-002D-4500
3 sizes included
8' x 8'   12' x 8'   16' x 8'
building height: 8'-2"
includes both concrete slab and wood deck on gravel base foundations
material list/instructions included

MARCELLA
The 8' x 7' overhead garage-style door makes entry with large equipment easy. Several windows add light to the interior, offering ease when trying to locate items inside.

PLAN #C20-002D-4521
192 square feet
width: 12'   depth: 16'
building height: 12'-5"
slab foundation
material list/instructions included

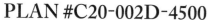
Blueprint PRICING and ORDERING + VISIT houseplansandmore.com + 1-800-373-2646

MERRILL
Attractive window boxes, operable windows, and a 2' deep front covered porch make this shed playhouse so charming! With a ceiling height of 6'-1", the kids will love it in warmer months.

PLAN #C20-002D-4505
64 square feet
width: 8'   depth: 8'
building height: 9'-2"
wood floor on 4x4 runners foundation
material list/instructions included

MARIANNA
This taller-style shed enjoys a barnyard look thanks to its Gambrel roof style. This shed would look great near your garden or anywhere on your property, especially in a rural setting.

PLAN #C20-002D-4501
includes 3 sizes
12' x 12'   12' x 16'   12' x 20'
building height: 12'-10"
slab foundation
material list/instructions included

SELLERSVILLE
This shed partners with adolescent fun time by offering a storage solution that can also be used as a children's playhouse, featuring a cute outdoor balcony.

PLAN #C20-002D-4514
144 square feet
width: 12'   depth: 12'
building height: 14'-1"
includes both concrete slab and wood deck on block pier foundations
material list/instructions included

MADDY
The perfect all-purpose shed design features a garage door style entry as well as another side entry door. Two windows brighten the interior superbly.

PLAN #C20-002D-4506
192 square feet
width: 16'   depth: 12'
building height: 12'-5"
slab foundation
material list/instructions included

Blueprint PRICING and ORDERING + VISIT houseplansandmore.com + 1-800-373-2646

RASMUSSEN
This charming barn-style shed matches true country style without a hitch. Double front doors and a Gambrel-style roof create an easy-to-use interior space.

PLAN #C20-002D-4520
120 square feet
width: 10'   depth: 12'
building height: 10'-7"
wood floor on 4x4 runners foundation
material list/instructions included

BOSCOBEL
Absolutely the perfect garden shed with plenty of light in the interior, providing an ideal place for seedlings to flourish in colder temperatures.

PLAN #C20-002D-4523
100 square feet
width: 10'   depth: 10'
building height: 11'-4"
wood floor on 4x4 runners foundation
material list/instructions included

BLONDELL
This classic shed style looks great in any backyard setting. Use it to store yard equipment, patio furniture in the off-season and gardening supplies.

PLAN #C20-002D-4504
includes 3 sizes:
10' x 12'   10' x 16'   10' x 20'
building height: 8'-9"
wood floor on 4x4 runners foundation
material list/instructions included

MAUDE
This garden shed has large skylight windows for optimal plant growth and ample room for tool and lawn equipment storage, too. Start enjoying your own organic veggies year-round with help from this handy shed!

PLAN #C20-002D-4507
120 square feet
width: 10'   depth: 12'
building height: 9'-9"
wood floor on gravel base foundation
material list/instructions included

CARMEN COVE
Available in three popular sizes, these mini barns provide an ample storage solution for your lawn or garden equipment and includes a 4' x 6'-4" double-door for easy access.

PLAN #C20-002D-4502
includes 3 sizes:
10' x 12'   10' x 16'   10' x 20'
building height: 8'-5"
wood floor on 4x4 runners foundation
material list/instructions included

HERNDON
This shed would make the best and most comfortable workshop. With its covered front porch and three windows, it would be the perfect spot for the family handyman to work without distractions!

PLAN #C20-002D-7520
width: 24'   depth: 20'
building height: 13'-6"
slab foundation
material list/instructions included

NOVAK
This economical and easy-to-build modern-inspired shed features a barn-style sliding door entry with a transom above for added light to the interior. The stylish solution for your storage needs!

PLAN #C20-165D-4502
192 square feet
width: 16'   depth: 12'
building height: 12'-6"
slab foundation

MARCIA
The Gambrel roof design on this storage shed gives it a pleasing country style. It allows easy access thanks to its 5'-6" x 6'-8" double-door entry.

PLAN #C20-002D-4508
includes 3 sizes:
12' x8'   12' x 12'   12' x 16'
building height: 9'-10"
includes both concrete slab and wood deck on concrete pier foundations
material list/instructions included

MARILYN
This cheerful shed with porch and firewood storage has a friendly double window brightening the interior. Designed to appear like a cottage, it has a convenient overhang, perfect for storing firewood.

PLAN #C20-125D-4501
122 square feet
width: 17'   depth: 12'
building height: 16'-10"
slab foundation

BOXWOOD
An attractive shed, ideal for providing stylish storage right in your backyard. Popular barn-style sliding doors make yard equipment and gardening supplies super easy to access.

PLAN #C20-165D-4501
160 square feet
width: 16'   depth: 10'
building height: 12'-3"
slab foundation

BLAINE
With a perfect 3' x 6'-8" Dutch-style door, this shed is ideal for storage or as a fun playhouse for children. Shutters and a window box create a charming exterior that will look great in any backyard.

PLAN #C20-002D-4522
72 square feet
width: 12' depth: 8'
building height: 10'-5"
wood floor on 4x4 runners foundation
material list/instructions included

SHAW
This sleek shed would look fantastic with any style of home, but especially with the modern farmhouse style. It would be the perfect spot for potting plants since it includes Double French doors and a window illuminating the interior perfectly for any task at hand.

PLAN #C20-165D-4500
420 square feet
width: 30' depth: 14'
building height: 12'-8"
slab foundation

Blueprint PRICING and ORDERING + VISIT houseplansandmore.com + 1-800-373-2646

PENNEY
The perfect rustic Craftsman shed offers a double-door entry into the inside for ease and also a covered front porch, making it a nice place to relax or store firewood in a dry, sheltered place.

PLAN #C20-142D-4501
150 square feet
width: 15' depth: 15'
building height: 14'
wood floor joists over treated girders foundation

JENNAR
With wide double-doors that open to the inside and its wraparound covered porch design, this shed is perfect for firewood storage. The decorative dormer adds light to the interior and great style to the exterior.

PLAN #C20-125D-4502
151 square feet
width: 19' depth: 17'
building height: 16'
slab foundation

NORRIS
An attractive-style shed that is perfect for storage of lawn and garden equipment, this shed also includes a 4' x 6' double-door for easy access.

PLAN #C20-002D-4524
includes 4 sizes:
8' x 8' 8' x 10' 8' x 12' 8' x 16"
building height: 7'-6"
wood floor on 4x4 runners foundation
material list/instructions included

ROSARIO HILL
This is the perfect option for the backyard of a Modern Farmhouse style home. It would make a great garden workshop or "she" shed with its barn style sliding doors for accessing cool breezes.

PLAN #C20-125D-4511
192 square feet
width: 16' depth: 12'
building height: 15'
slab foundation

RICHMANN
The Richmann is a stylish shed that looks great with Modern Farmhouse architecture. It's an ideal choice for a tractor or other yard equipment.

PLAN #C20-113D-4514
309 square feet
width: 20' depth: 15'-5"
building height: 15'-10"
monolithic slab foundation

VERNON
The perfect little Modern Farmhouse-inspired shed has both a single door entry and a double door entry into the two-story tall storage space.

PLAN #C20-125D-4507
292 square feet
width: 22' depth: 16'
building height: 24'
slab foundation

HOW CAN I FIND OUT IF I CAN AFFORD TO BUILD?

GET AN ACCURATE ESTIMATED COST-TO-BUILD REPORT

The most important question for someone wanting to build a home or outdoor project is, "How much is it going to cost?" Obviously, you must have an accurate budget set prior to ordering plans and beginning construction, or your project will quickly turn into a nightmare. Our goal is to make building your home or project a much simpler reality that's within reach, thanks to the estimated cost-to-build report available for all of the plans in this book and on our website, houseplansandmore.com.

Price is always the number-one factor when selecting a new home. Price dictates the size and the quality of materials you will choose. So, it comes as no surprise that having an accurate building estimate prior to making your final decision on a home or project plan is quite possibly the most important step in the entire process.

If you feel you've found "the" plan, then before taking the step of purchasing plans, order an estimated cost-to-build report for the zip code where you want to build. When you order this report created specifically for you, it will educate you on all costs associated with building your new home or project. Simply order the cost-to-build report on houseplansandmore.com for the home you want to build and gain knowledge of the material and labor cost associated with the home. Not only does the report allow you to choose the quality of the materials, you can also select options in every aspect of the project, from lot condition to contractor fees. This report will allow you to successfully manage your construction budget in all areas, clearly see where the majority of the costs lie, and save you money from start to finish.

Listed below are the categories included in every cost-to-build report (if applicable). Each category breaks down labor cost, material cost, and funds needed, and the report offers the ability to manipulate over/under-adjustments if necessary.

BASIC INFORMATION includes your contact information, the state and zip code where you intend to build. First, select material class. It will include details of the home such as square footage, number of windows, fireplaces, balconies, and bathrooms. Deck, basement, or bonus room square footage is included. Lot size and garage location and number of bays are also included.

GENERAL SOFT COSTS include cost for plans, customizing (if applicable), building permits, pre-construction services, and planning expenses.

SITE WORK & UTILITIES include water, sewer, electric, and gas. Choose the type of site work you will need prior to building and if you'll need a driveway.

FOUNDATION is selected from a menu that lists the most common types.

FRAMING ROUGH SHELL calculates your rough framing costs, including framing for fireplaces, balconies, decks, porches, basements, and bonus rooms.

ROOFING includes several options so you can see how it will affect your overall price.

DRY OUT SHELL allows you to select doors, windows, siding and garage doors.

ELECTRICAL includes wiring and the quality of the light fixtures.

PLUMBING includes plumbing materials, plumbing fixtures, and fireproofing materials. It includes labor costs and the ability to change fixture quality.

HVAC includes costs for both labor and materials.

INSULATION includes costs for both labor and materials.

FINISH SHELL includes drywall, interior doors and trim, stairs, shower doors, mirrors, and bath accessories - costs for both labor and materials.

CABINETS & VANITIES select the grade of your cabinets, vanities, kitchen countertops, and bathroom vanity materials, as well as appliances.

PAINTING includes all painting materials, their quality, and labor.

FLOORING includes over a dozen flooring material options.

SPECIAL EQUIPMENT NEEDS calculate cost for unforeseen expenses.

CONTRACTOR FEE / PROJECT MANAGER includes the cost of your cost-to-build report, project manager, and/or general contractor fees. If you're doing the managing yourself, your costs will be tremendously lower in this portion.

LAND PAYOFF includes the cost of your land.

RESERVES/CLOSING COSTS includes interest, contingency reserves, and closing costs.

We've taken the guesswork out of what your project will cost. Take control of your project, determine major expenses upfront, and save money. Easily supervise all costs, from labor to materials. Manage construction with confidence and avoid costly mistakes and unforeseen expenses. To order a cost-to-build report for a home, visit houseplansandmore.com and search for the plan number. Then, look for the button that says "Request Your Report" and get started. If you're interested in a cost-to-build report for a garage or shed, then call us at 1-800-373-2646 and we will assist you.

OUR BLUEPRINT PACKAGES INCLUDE

FIND OUT WHAT IS TYPICALLY INCLUDED

A quality home – one that looks good, functions well, and provides years of enjoyment – is a product of many things: design, materials, and craftsmanship. But it's also the result of outstanding blueprints – the actual plans and specifications that tell the builder exactly how to build your home.

And with our **BLUEPRINT PACKAGES** you get the absolute best. A complete set of blueprints is available for every design in this book. These "working drawings" are highly detailed, resulting in two key benefits:

- BETTER UNDERSTANDING BY THE CONTRACTOR OF HOW TO BUILD YOUR HOME AND...

- MORE ACCURATE CONSTRUCTION ESTIMATES THAT WILL SAVE YOU TIME AND MONEY.

Below is a description of the plan information included for most of the designs in this book. Specific details may vary with each designer's plan. While this information is typical for most plans, we cannot assure the inclusion of all the following referenced items.

Please contact us at 1-800-373-2646 for a specific plan's information.

COVER SHEET is the artist's rendering of the home's exterior. It gives you an idea of how the home will look when finished.

FOUNDATION plan shows the layout of the specific foundation type you've chosen with all notations and dimensions included. See the specific plan page for the foundation types available. If a home plan doesn't have your desired foundation type, please call 1-800-373-2646 and we'll advise you on how to customize the plan to include the foundation you need.

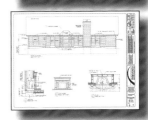

FLOOR PLANS show wall placement, doors, closets, plumbing fixtures, electrical outlets, columns, and beams.

INTERIOR ELEVATIONS provide views of interior elements such as fireplaces, kitchen cabinets, built-in units, and other features of the home.

EXTERIOR ELEVATIONS illustrate the front, rear, and sides of the house and include the required dimensions and exterior material details.

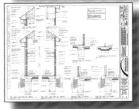

SECTIONS show detailed views of the home or portions of the home as if it were sliced from the roof to the foundation. This shows load-bearing walls, stairs, joists, trusses, and other structural elements.

DETAILS show how to construct certain components such as the roof system, stairs, deck, etc.

WHAT KIND OF PLAN PACKAGE DO YOU NEED?

SELECT THE TYPE OF BLUEPRINT THAT BEST FITS YOUR SITUATION

Please note: Not all plan packages and options listed below are available for every plan. There may be additional options available; please visit houseplansandmore.com, or call 1-800-373-2646 for all current pricing and options. The plan package and option pricing shown in this book is subject to change without notice.

1-SET PLAN PACKAGE includes one complete set of construction drawings. Typically you'll need one set for yourself so additional sets of blueprints may be required for your lender, your local building department, your contractor, and any other tradespeople working on your project. Please note: This one set of plans is copyrighted, so it can't be altered or copied.

5-SET PLAN PACKAGE includes five complete sets of construction drawings. Besides one set for yourself, additional sets of blueprints will be required for your lender, your local building department, your contractor, and any other tradespeople working on your project. Please note: These 5 sets of plans are copyrighted, so they can't be altered or copied.

8-SET PLAN PACKAGE includes eight complete sets of construction drawings. Besides one set for yourself, additional sets of blueprints will be required for your lender, your local building department, your contractor, and any other tradespeople working on your project. Please note: These 8 sets of plans are copyrighted, so they can't be altered or copied.

PDF FILE FORMAT is our most popular plan option because of how fast you can receive them (usually within 24 to 48 hours Monday through Friday), and their ability to be easily shared via email with your contractor, subcontractors, and local building officials. The PDF file format is a complete set of construction drawings in an electronic file format. It includes a one-time build copyright release that allows you to make changes and copies of the plans. Typically you will receive a PDF file via email within 24-48 hours (Mon-Fri, 7:30am-4:30pm CST), allowing you to save money on shipping. Upon receiving, visit a local copy or print shop and print the number of plans you need to build your home, or print one and alter the plan by using correction fluid and drawing in your modifications. Please note: These are flat image files and cannot be altered electronically. PDF files are nonrefundable and not returnable.

CAD FILE FORMAT is the actual computer files for a plan directly from AutoCAD or another computer-aided design program. CAD files are the best option if you have a significant amount of changes to make to the plan or if you need to make the plan fit your local codes. If you purchase a CAD file, it allows you or a local design professional the ability to modify the plans electronically in a CAD program, so making changes to the plan is easier and less expensive than using a paper set of plans when modifying. A CAD package also includes a one-time build copyright release that allows you to legally make your changes, and print multiple copies of the plan. See houseplansandmore.com for availability and pricing. Please note: CAD files are nonrefundable and not returnable.

MIRROR REVERSE SETS Sometimes a home fits a site better if it is flipped left to right. A mirror reverse set of plans is simply a mirror image of the original drawings, causing the lettering and dimensions to read backwards. Therefore, when ordering a mirror reverse set of plans, you must purchase at least one set of the original plans to read from, and use the mirror reverse set for construction. Some plans offer right-reading reverse for an additional fee. This means the plan has been redrawn by the designer as the mirrored version and can easily be read.

ADDITIONAL SETS You can order additional sets of a plan for an additional fee. A 5-set or 8-set plan package must have been previously purchased. Please note: Only available within 90 days after purchase of a plan package.

2" X 6" EXTERIOR WALLS 2" x 6" exterior walls can be purchased for some plans for an additional fee (see houseplansandmore.com for availability and pricing).

DO YOU WANT TO MAKE CHANGES TO YOUR PLAN?

We understand that sometimes it is difficult to find blueprints that meet all of your specific needs. That is why we offer plan modification services so you can build a plan exactly the way you want it!

ARE YOU THINKING ABOUT CUSTOMIZING A PLAN?

If you're like many customers, you want to make changes to the your home or project plan you've chosen to make it how you've always wanted. That's where our expert design and modification partners come in. You won't find a more efficient and economic way to get your changes done than by using our customizing services.

Whether it's enlarging a kitchen, adding a porch, or converting a crawl space to a basement, we can customize any plan and make it perfect for you. Simply create your wish list and let us go to work. Soon you'll have the customized blueprints for your plan, and at a fraction of the cost of hiring a local architect!

IT'S EASY!

- We can customize any plan in this book.
- We provide a FREE cost estimate for your home plan modifications within 24-48 hours (Monday-Friday, 7:30am-4:30pm CST).
- Average turn-around time to complete the modifications is typically 4-5 weeks.
- You will receive one-on-one design consultations.

CUSTOMIZING FACTS

- The average cost to have a plan customized is typically less than 1% of the building costs - compare that to the national average of 7% of building costs.
- The average modification cost for a home is typically $800 to $1,500. This does not include the cost of purchasing the PDF file format of the blueprints, which is required to legally make the plan modifications.

OTHER HELPFUL INFO

- Sketch or make a specific list of changes you'd like to make on the Plan Modification Request Form.
- A plan modification specialist will contact you within 1-2 business days with your free estimate.
- Upon accepting the estimate, you will need to purchase the PDF or CAD file format.
- A contract, which includes a specific list of changes and fees, will be sent to you prior for your approval.
- Upon approval, your modification specialist will keep you informed by emailing sketches of the project.
- Plans can be converted to metric, or to a Barrier-free layout (also referred to as a universal home design, which allows easier mobility for an individual with limitations of any kind).

2 EASY STEPS

1 VISIT houseplansandmore.com and click on the Resources tab at the top of the home page, or scan the QR code to the left to download the Plan Modification Request Form.

2 EMAIL your completed form to: customizehpm@designamerica.com.
  If you're unable to access the Internet, please call us at 1-800-373-2646
  (Monday-Friday, 7:30am - 4:30pm CST).

OTHER HELPFUL BUILDING AIDS

Your blueprints will contain all of the necessary construction information you need to build your home. But, we also offer the following products and services to save you time and money in the building process.

MATERIAL LIST Many of the home plans in this book have a material list available for purchase that gives you the quantity, dimensions, and description of the building materials needed to construct the home (see houseplansandmore.com for availability and pricing). Keep in mind, due to variations in local building code requirements, exact material quantities cannot be guaranteed.

Please note: Material lists are created with the standard foundation type only. Please review the material list and the construction drawings with your material supplier to verify measurements and quantities of the material listed before ordering supplies.

THE LEGAL KIT Avoid many legal pitfalls and build your home with confidence using the forms and contracts featured in this kit. Included are request for proposal documents, various fixed price and cost plus contracts, instructions on how and when to use each form, warranty statements, and more. Save time and money before you break ground on your new home or start a remodeling project. All forms are reproducible. This kit is ideal for homebuilders and contractors.

Cost: $35

DETAIL PLAN PACKAGES -

ELECTRICAL, FRAMING & PLUMBING Three separate packages offer homebuilders details for constructing various foundations; numerous floor, wall, and roof framing techniques; simple to complex residential wiring; sump and water softener hookups; plumbing connection methods; installation of septic systems; and more. Each package includes three-dimensional illustrations and a glossary of terms.

Purchase one or all three. Cost: $30 each, or all three for $60. Please note: These drawings do not pertain to a specific home plan, but they include general guidelines and tips for construction in all three of these trades.

EXPRESS DELIVERY Most orders are processed within 24 hours of receipt. Please allow 7-10 business days for standard delivery. If you need to place a rush order, please call us by 11:00am Monday-Friday CST and ask for express service (allow 1-2 business days).

Please see page 238 for specific pricing information for shipping and handling.

TECHNICAL ASSISTANCE If you have questions about your blueprints, we offer technical assistance by calling 1-314-770-2228 (Monday-Friday, 7:30am-4:30pm CST). Whether it involves design modifications or field assistance, our home plans team is extremely familiar with all of our designs and will be happy to help you. We want your home to be everything you expect it to be.

BEFORE YOU ORDER

Please note: Plan package and plan option pricing are subject to change without notice. For current pricing, visit houseplansandmore.com or call us at 1-800-373-2646.

BUILDING CODE REQUIREMENTS At the time the construction drawings were prepared, every effort was made to ensure that these plans and specifications met nationally recognized codes. These plans conform to most national building codes. Because building codes vary from area to area, some drawing modifications and/or the assistance of a professional designer or architect may be necessary to comply with your local codes or to accommodate your specific building site conditions. We advise you to consult with your local building official or a local builder for information regarding codes governing your area prior to ordering blueprints.

COPYRIGHT Plans are protected under Copyright Law. Reproduction by any means is strictly prohibited. The right of building only one structure from all plan packages is licensed exclusively to the buyer, and the plans may not be resold unless by express written authorization from the home designer or architect. You may not use this design to build a second or multiple structure(s) without purchasing a multi-build license. Each violation of the copyright law is punishable by a fine.

LICENSE TO BUILD When you purchase a "full set of construction drawings" from Design America, Inc., you are purchasing an exclusive one-time "License to Build," not the rights to the design. Design America, Inc.," is granting you permission on behalf of the plan's designer or architect to use the construction drawings one time for the building of the home. The construction drawings (also referred to as blueprints/plans and any derivative of that plan, whether extensive or minor) are still owned and protected under copyright laws by the original designer. The blueprints/plans cannot be resold, transferred, rented, loaned, or used by anyone other than the original purchaser of the "License to Build" without written consent from Design America, Inc., or the plan designer. If you are interested in building the plan more than once, please call 1-800-373-2646 and inquire about purchasing a Multi-Build License that will allow you to build a home design more than one time.

Please note: A "full set of construction drawings" consists of either CAD files or PDF files.

EXCHANGE POLICY Since blueprints are printed in response to your order, we cannot honor requests for refunds.

SHIPPING & HANDLING CHARGES

U.S. SHIPPING
(AK and HI express only)

Regular (allow 7-10 business days)	$30.00
Priority (allow 3-5 business days)	$50.00
Express* (allow 1-2 business days)	$75.00

CANADA SHIPPING**

Regular (allow 8-12 business days)	$50.00
Express* (allow 3-5 business days)	$100.00

OVERSEAS SHIPPING/INTERNATIONAL

For shipping costs, please call or email (customerservice@designamerica.com)

* For express delivery please call us by 11:00am Monday-Friday CST

** Orders may be subject to custom's fees and or duties/taxes.

Note: Shipping & handling does not apply on PDF and CAD File orders. PDF and CAD orders will be emailed within 24-48 hours (Monday - Friday, 7:30am - 4:30pm CST) of purchase.

ORDER FORM

PLEASE NOTE: Plan package and plan option pricing are subject to change without notice. For current pricing, visit houseplansandmore.com, or call us at 1-800-373-2646.

Please send me the following:

Plan Number: C20-_____

Select Foundation Type:

(Select ONE- see plan page for available options).

☐ Slab   ☐ Crawl space   ☐ Basement

☐ Walk-out basement   ☐ Pier

☐ Optional foundation for an additional fee

    Enter additional foundation cost $_____

PLAN PACKAGE   COST

☐ CAD File $_____

☐ PDF File Format (recommended) $_____

☐ 8-Set Plan Package $_____

☐ 5-Set Plan Package $_____

☐ 1-Set Plan Package $_____

Visit houseplansandmore.com to see current pricing and all plan package options available.

IMPORTANT EXTRAS

For all plan options, current pricing and availability, visit houseplansandmore.com, or call 1-800-373-2646.

☐ Additional plan sets*:

    _____ set(s) at $_____ per set $_____

☐ Print in mirror reverse:

    _____ set(s) at $_____ per set $_____

    (where right-reading reverse is not available)

☐ Print in right-reading reverse:

    one-time additional fee of $_____ $_____

☐ Material List $_____

☐ Legal Kit (001D-9991, see page 237) $_____

Detail Plan Packages: (see page 237)

    ☐ Framing   ☐ Electrical   ☐ Plumbing $_____

    (001D-9992)   (001D-9993)   (001D-9994)

Shipping (see page 238) $_____

SUBTOTAL $_____

Sales Tax (MO residents only, add 8.24%) $_____

TOTAL $_____

*Available only within 90 days after purchase of plan

HELPFUL TIPS

- You can upgrade to a different plan package within 90 days of your original plan purchase.
- Additional sets cannot be ordered without the purchase of 5-Sets or 8-Sets.

Name _____

             (Please print or type)

Street _____

         (Please do not use a P.O. Box)

City _____

State _____

Country _____ Zip _____

Daytime telephone _(_____)_____

E-Mail _____

      (For invoice and tracking info)

<u>Payment</u>   ☐ Bank check/money order.

         No personal checks.

Make check/money order payable to Design America, Inc.

☐ MasterCard   ☐ VISA   ☐ DISCOVER   ☐ AMERICAN EXPRESS Cards

Credit card number _____

Expiration date (mm/yy) _____

CID _____

Signature _____

☐ I hereby authorize Design America, Inc., to charge this purchase to my credit card.

Please check the appropriate box:

☐ Building home for myself

☐ I'm building the home for someone else

ORDER ONLINE houseplansandmore.com

ORDER BY PHONE

1-800-373-2646   Fax: 314-770-2226

ORDER BY MAIL

Design America, Inc.
734 West Port Plaza, Suite #208
St. Louis, MO 63146

EXPRESS DELIVERY

Most orders are processed within 24 hours of receipt. If you need to place a rush order, please call us by 11:00am CST and ask for express service.

Business Hours: Monday-Friday (7:30am-4:30pm CST)

Cozy Cottage & Cabin Designs

SOURCE CODE C20

INDEX

PHOTO CREDITS

Unless noted below, all photos and images throughout this publication are copyrighted by the designer/architect; page 2, photo featuring home by REAL LOG HOMES®, realloghomes.com, photographer Roger Wade Studios; page 3, photo courtesy of REAL LOG HOMES®, realloghomes.com, photographer James Ray Spahn; page 4, photo courtesy of REAL LOG HOMES®, realloghomes.com, photographer James Ray Spahn; page 6, bottom, left: Plan #011S-0206 at houseplansandmore.com; page 7, REAL LOG HOMES®, realloghomes.com, photographer James Ray Spahn; page 9, photo courtesy of REAL LOG HOMES®, realloghomes.com, photographer Roger Wade Studios; page 44, photo courtesy of nextluxury.com; page 4, top: photo courtesy of signaturehardware.com; bottom: Plan #028D-0115 on page 38; page 47, photo courtesy of blesserhouse.com; page 48, photo courtesy of ClosetMaid®; page 103, photo courtesy of R-Control® SIPs; page 123, bottom right: photo courtesy of REAL LOG HOMES®, realloghomes.com, photographer James Ray Spahn; page 161 bottom, #142D-7500 on page 164; bottom: courtesy of ClosetMaid®; page 163, Plan #173D-7500 on page 166; page 178, top, right: courtesy of ClosetMaid®; bottom, right: courtesy of istockphoto; page 179, top, left: courtesy of istockphoto; bottom: courtesy of REAL LOG HOMES®, realloghomes.com, Photographer Rich Frutchey; page 181, photo courtesy of REAL LOG HOMES®, realloghomes.com, photographer James Ray Spahn; page 202, top, Plan #C20-002D-4506 on page 227, bottom, left and right, plan #C20-002D-4515 on page 225, photos courtesy of CPI, Black & Decker; page 203, both photos courtesy of CPI, Black & Decker.